HACKING EXECUTIVE LEADERSHIP

Published by Advantage Publishing Group

978-1-954024-13-7 Hardcover
978-1-954024-14-4 Paperback
978-1-954024-15-1 Ebook

https://nextlevel.coach
To contact, please e-mail: emily@nextlevel.coach

HACKING EXECUTIVE LEADERSHIP

Go from insecure, indecisive, and overloaded to confident, influential, and effective

By
Emily Sander

DEDICATION

To Mom, Dad, and Chris

CONTENTS

INTRODUCTION

Reading this book can change your life.

How many times have you heard that before? Too many times to count, right? So, let me try something else.

Maybe I can read your mind a little. You picked up a book called *Hacking Executive Leadership*, so I'm guessing you're a high achiever. You've done well in your field through a combination of talent and sheer drive. You're hungry to get better and believe that self-improvement is a life-long endeavor.

You consider yourself a creative thinker, and your brain is always swirling with new ideas. Maybe too many ideas...You also find yourself getting jumbled and overwhelmed and you don't know where to start.

One of my clients came to me, saying, "It's like I'm in a forest. I can't see anything. I don't even know where I am. What trees am I supposed to cut down? In what direction? What's the best way to cut them? Do I even need to chop them down?"

Or does this sound familiar? A critical decision must be made, and everyone is looking to you. Cue images of everything bad that might happen if you make the wrong call, followed by the predictable knot in the pit of your stomach. You're tempted to delay the decision or avoid it altogether.

What if you could take a magic pill and never second-guess yourself again?

Imagine leading with confidence every time.

Or maybe, you've been around the block once or twice and you keep running into the same personal roadblocks. As an executive or entrepreneur, you don't necessarily answer to anyone, but you know that you could, and should, be more effective at optimizing your time.

Another client, the founder of two companies, thought she needed help staying on track with her day-to-day tasks. "I know 401ks and things like that are important," she said, "but I'd rather stab my eyes out, so I keep putting them off." I helped her see that she was trying to lean her ladder on the wrong wall.

Like the first runner in a relay race, she was great at getting out of the blocks; she was without a doubt, a great sprinter. She excelled when it comes to generating great ideas, having a strategic vision and starting a successful company. Yet, she had no interest in the later legs of the race, in cultivating the business after it had bloomed. It was a dream come true, for both my client and her Chief Operating Officer, when she handed the baton off to the next person. The COO got to run the company while my client got to start another race!

What if the solution to many of your problems was a simple as putting on a pair of glasses?

After rising quickly through the ranks of corporate America and leading customer-focused teams at small-to-medium SaaS companies, I've discovered that the right framework is the most important predictor of success. Not only that, but the right framework can easily give you the biggest bang for your buck.

I love coaching. I'm truly grateful to work with business leaders from all around the world. My corporate track record, paired with my experience of coaching numerous executives to get to the next level, means that I can help you with the challenges—and opportunities! —that you're facing.

You don't need to be afraid anymore. You don't need to constantly be in firefighting mode. This book is filled with strategies and tools for taking control over your life and your career. I don't care if you're a high-potential individual, an early executive looking for a head start, or a seasoned executive. If you have a growth mindset and are looking to up your game and gain an edge, this book is a goldmine.

You will become a better, more effective leader. You will not only learn to make little adjustments, but you will also gain new perspectives and tools that will take you to the next level and make you the epitome of self-improvement to those around you.

I know you're busy, but who do you want to be in a week, a month, or a year from now? The same person, with the same challenges? Someone that missed out on a life-changing opportunity?

So many people have the "I'll do it tomorrow," mindset and it is a crippling one. They put things off until "tomorrow," but tomorrow never actually comes. Don't let tomorrow turn into "later" or "one day." Time flies, and the compound effect will either be in your favor or to your detriment. Invest in yourself today. Step into your next level of leadership.

So, seize the moment and turn the page.

PART ONE

THE FRAMEWORK

Part one provides the foundation for how you collect, structure, and filter information and experiences.

CHAPTER 1

"FAILURE"

"Feedback is the breakfast of Champions."

- Ken Blanchard

"Winning is great, sure, but if you are really going to do something in life, the secret is learning how to lose. Nobody goes undefeated all the time. If you can pick up after a crushing defeat, and go on to win again, you are going to be a champion someday."

- Wilma Rudolph

What do you think of when you hear the word "fail"? How many things have you "failed" in the past? What comes to mind when you think about potentially "failing" at something in the future?

Probably negative words, thoughts, or connotations, right?

Everyone has "failed" at something at one point or another. Almost everyone has felt that dark pit of failure in their stomach. Once this feeling sinks in, most people tend to quit in order to avoid feeling this way. They then turn around and call themselves a failure and unfortunately, some people let it define them. These events and reactions can hold so many people back.

Executives need to have a special relationship with the concept of "failing." You will be doing more of this as you move up and take on more responsibility. As such, you will need to become increasingly better at working with failure in order to be the most successful leader you can be.

Executives make tough decisions every day, which means they need to have a high-risk tolerance. They need to be confident and know that they will be able to handle any situation. Learning ways to "fail forward" will allow you to be a more decisive and effective leader.

The reason only a subset of people do this well is because a powerful emotion is involved. Fear. At the root of not wanting to fail is fear - "I'm scared I'll mess up. I'm scared I'll make the wrong decision. I'm scared everyone will see and think less of me. I'm afraid I'll let people down."

You're scared of the *feeling* that often accompanies failure. And, this makes sense because it can feel...well, shitty. A lot of people talk about overcoming fear in big, lofty philosophical terms. These can sound great beforehand and are even credible theories, but when life kicks you in a special place, it becomes a whole different ballgame. There is a lot of growth and wisdom that can only come from failure; however, it does not diminish the fact that failing is a difficult pill to swallow.

I'll shoot it to you straight - you will always feel the fear. I can't guarantee that you won't feel a little bad when things don't turn out the way you want or expect, but don't slam the book shut just yet!

Because if you turn "failure" into progress, then you can never fail again. Well, not in the true sense anyways. Failure is only real failure if you *stop*. If you sit on the ground, throw your hands up, and declare you've been defeated forever.

Failure has been in quotes up to this point because what most people consider failure is *actually* progress in the making. This may be unpleasant to hear but sometimes failure is a necessary stepping stone to success. Oftentimes, constant failure is an indicator of a driven, successful person. Whenever someone says the word failure, I put quotes around it in my head. Feel free to do the same.

Now, let's move forward and talk about ways to transform the fear of failure into the anticipation of progress, which starts with knowing where you currently stand in the overall process.

Know Where You Are in the Process

Having perspective is helpful in almost any situation, and the same can be said for failure. We all get so wrapped up in our own minds that we often suffer from severe tunnel vision. Instead of focusing on the big picture, we cannot see past what's right in front of us. Simply having the awareness of what the process is and where you are in it, will give you some peace of mind.

Here is a visual representation of failure:

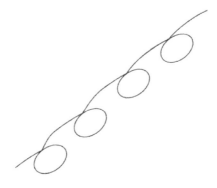

"Failure" framework. Transform failure into progress by looping up.

This chart showcases the path to progress and achieving goals. Notice how it is not a straight line. Instead, it's a series of connected loops on an upward slope. The overall chain of loops goes up and to the right. Yet, it's made up of a series of individual loops - or "failures." With each loop, there is a point where the line is indeed curving back downwards. It's going down and to the left - the opposite direction of progress. But only for a little bit, it's temporary. If learning and improvement are applied, it *loops back up* and continues upward.

I feel it is important to reiterate this point: *It. Loops. Back. Up.*

The overall trajectory continues up and to the right, and then it will encounter another individual loop, go back down, and then continue its steady march onward.

In this next picture, you can see the part of the loop where life can kick you right in the feels.

"Failure" Framework. Keep perspective when you are in this part of the process.

The steepest part of the downward side of the loop is where you realize something has not gone the way you had planned. This is when you have to admit to other people your plans went awry. You also have to admit it to yourself and figure out what the hell you're going to do now. In almost all scenarios, your inner critic will blare its nonsense over your internal PA system.

Many people get stuck in the downward part of the loop. They think that's the end, so they stop trying. However, if they kept going, they would have eventually looped back up and continue to the next stage of progress.

The trick is to first identify your misstep and then apply the lesson you learned from this specific experience to your future choices. Easier said than done, I know. In these moments, remember that, as painful as it is, *there's valuable information that has been gained.* This part of the process is where champions are made. And if applied correctly, it will be what you need in order to propel yourself back up the loop.

Quote: *"You have to look at the reality of the situation. You kind of got to get over yourself... Okay, you feel embarrassed. You're not that important. Get over yourself. You're worried about how people may perceive you and like you're walking around because it's embarrassing because you shot five air balls. Get over yourself.*

And then after that, well, it's why did those air balls happen? [I] Got it. [In] High school, [the] year before, we played 35 games, max. [There was a] Week in between, spaced out, plenty of times to rest. In the NBA it's back-to-back-to-back. I didn't have the legs. If you look at the shots. Every shot was on line. But every shot was short.

I got to get stronger. I got to train differently. The weight training program that I'm doing, I got to tailor it for an 82-game season so that when the playoffs come around my legs are stronger and that ball gets there. So, I look at it with rationale. Ok, so, well, the reason I shot air balls is because my legs aren't there. Next year they'll be there. That was it. Done."

- Kobe Bryant

In order to truly learn from your mistakes, you must first be brave enough to face what just happened. It might even mean that you will have to dig through the muck of what *you* did to contribute to the unsuccessful situation. This is never fun, but it is imperative. Why? Because you are the only variable that you have control over in any given situation. What can you take away from this that will be helpful to you in the future? If you are willing to do the work at this stage, then you already standout from the crowd since the majority of people refuse to put in the work. Remember, do the work.

> **Quote:** *"I'm going to do today what other people aren't willing to, so I can do tomorrow what other people can't."*
>
> *- Mat Fraser, CrossFit Champion*

Once you have a better understanding of the process and where you currently stand, it is important to keep some strategies in mind in order to loop back up.

It's Practice

One way to look at failure or the spot at the bottom part of the loop is to view it as practice. It's practice for the next time. It's practice for *all* the times in the future.

If a concert pianist wants to become world-class, he knows it will take a lot of practice—countless hours of failing and not playing the notes perfectly. Let's imagine two pianists who both share the same dream of making it big.

The first pianist is Pianist A. Each time he makes a mistake, he hates himself for it because he feels ashamed. He then berates himself for messing up and then he runs away from the piano. He no longer finds joy in practicing and only plays when he is forced to do so.

Now, imagine Pianist B. Each time *he* makes a mistake, he also feels disappointed that he didn't hit the right note. Yet, instead of sitting in his brooding feelings, he decides to analyze the situation. He pauses, takes a few seconds to think about what happened and why. Did he hit the wrong note because he was not paying attention? Or did he mess up with his left hand because he is right-handed? Once he figures out why he missed a certain note, he thinks of different ways to do it better next time.

Out of the two pianists, who do you think is going to make the most progress?

Whose experience is going to be more pleasant?

Who is going to get the most out of their time?

Pianist B will go further.

> **Pro Tip**: *Remember, failure is a reflection of something that happened, it does not define who you are as a person. It is important to note the difference between being disappointed in an outcome versus questioning your self-worth.*

The more you sink your teeth into your practice sessions, the more you'll get out of it. In Daniel Coyle's book, *The Talent Code*, he talks about how remarkable people from all fields have a different way of practicing. He calls it "deep practice."

The notion of deep practice is not just simply going through the motions, and it's not just putting in the time. It's operating at the edge of your ability and being *intentional with what you are doing.* Coyle notes, "When you're practicing deeply, the world's usual rules are suspended. You use time more efficiently. Your small efforts produce big, lasting results. You have positioned yourself at the place of leverage where you can capture failure and turn it into skill."

Use this leverage point to your advantage. Optimize this growth opportunity. Get the most out of the practice session.

Turn the Volume Down

While you are at the bottom part of the loop, remember that your *internal experience* is different from the *external ones.* Meaning, what you perceive to be happening - and particularly the weight and significance you give it - may differ greatly from what other people perceive.

A good example of this is public speaking. When people are nervous, they tend to be in their heads a lot. A speaker may feel like since he was so nervous, that his voice must have cracked several times. The first time it happened, he was so embarrassed that he took a long time to compose himself. The second time it happened, he cleared his throat so loudly that it distracted everyone. The third and probably the worst time, he had to walk across the entire stage to get a drink of water. At that point, everyone knew he was a horrible speaker. This whole scenario can be seen as the speaker's *internal experience*. Can you imagine him after his speech? He is probably sitting backstage with his head in his hands, sweating, and muttering about how awful his presentation had gone.

Now, imagine how different the same scenario played in the minds of the audience. If you were to ask different audience members how the presentation went, you will receive a range of responses:

- "That was a great presentation. I feel inspired!"
- "No, I didn't notice any nervousness from the speaker. Which part are you referring to?"
- "He seemed like an experienced speaker. He even emphasized his main point by pausing to get a drink of water. Good tactic."
- "Yeah, I heard him clear his throat. That's what you do when you speak sometimes."
- "I did see him stumble a little bit in that one section, but I loved how he regrouped and carried on - I'm going to try keep this tactic in mind the next time I have to give a presentation."
- "Yes, I saw his voice waver a little bit there which was such a relief because he always seems so put together and does everything so perfectly. I'm glad he's human too!"

These descriptions are the *external experience* of the audience.

Sometimes you need to remember to *turn down the volume* on your internal experience.

There is a difference - and often a pretty wide gulf - between your inner experience and the external perceptions of others.

> **Quote:** *"A feeling can't kill you...it's just a feeling...what I'm really afraid of is skiing..."*
>
> *- Julianne Moore, Actress*

> **Pro Tip:** *As you turn down the volume, it's easier to get into a more neutral headspace. One question to ask when all sorts of thoughts are popping up is, "Is this helpful?"*

Most people ask themselves, "Is this true?" Something might be true, yet it might not be helpful to dwell on. If you break your leg, it's true that the recovery process might be long and arduous. But, it's unhelpful to ruminate on that. Instead, it's helpful to focus on what you need to do that day in physical therapy.

Trevor Moawad is a mental conditioning expert who works with pro athletes and top-level CEOs. He espouses neutral thinking. A great example he recounts is the Apollo 13 space mission. This mission was supposed to take three American astronauts to the moon and back. Instead, an oxygen tank unexpectedly burst and damaged the spacecraft putting the mission and lives of the astronauts in jeopardy. The initial bang from the explosion prompted the famous words, "Houston, we have a problem."

Subsequently, the three astronauts asked a series of neutral questions around things like what part of the spacecraft did the issue occur, do we have enough oxygen, do we have enough water, is our trajectory correct to get back to earth? These were very significant questions, with life-or-death answers. But the astronauts meticulously worked through each step of the problem with a neutral mindset to get to a solution. They didn't become distraught over what just happened or what might happen. They focused on the very next step. If you want a taste of their level of calmness and professionalism, watch their post flight press conference. It's available on YouTube. The crew talks through the entire flight and the sequence of decisions and events that brought them safely home.

A Little Hypocritical, Aren't We?

When you're in the throes of feeling like a failure, it's easy to look back and see nothing but the negative. *Why did I do that? I can't believe I didn't see that. How could I be so stupid?*

We can be our harshest critics. It can be difficult or damn near impossible to have an objective opinion about ourselves at this stage.

Ask yourself, "What would I tell a friend in this situation?"

Pick someone you genuinely like and constantly root for. If this person came to you and were in the same situation you are in, what would you think? What would you notice? What would you say to him/her? Would you ever dream of telling this person the same things you're telling yourself?

It's *shocking* how differently we talk to ourselves versus how we talk to our friends and family members.

> **Pro Tip**: Ask a friend, a trusted colleague, or coach for their input.

Are you applying the same criteria and standards to yourself as you would a good friend?

Holding yourself to high standards is one thing but holding yourself to the unrealistic standard of perfection is another.

Raise your hand if you've performed flawlessly at everything your entire life. You have never taken a single step in the wrong direction; you make the exact right decision every time, and you continue to step into each moment and interaction perfectly. No matter who you ask this question to, there will be zero hands raised.

Imagine watching a baby learn how to walk. Who is going to watch the baby fall and then immediately walk over to its mother and exclaim, "Excuse me, but your baby just failed at walking; how could she be so stupid? How could you not see that? Why haven't you trained her better?" How many people have done this? Again, the answer here should be zero.

If you have ever fallen down or if you do not perform perfectly every time, then welcome to the club. Welcome to being human.

Growth and perfection can't co-exist.

Run Your Race

Avoid comparing yourself to others. This advice is good to keep in mind anytime, but it is especially crucial when you're hanging out at the bottom part of your loop. More specifically, try to avoid comparing yourself to the *outward appearance* of other people. They may appear to have it all together, to be at the pinnacle of their success, to look immaculate on a magazine cover or on a social media post, or they may sound on top of the world during an interview. It's easy to get sucked into a pity party for one. Logically, you know that these people have self-doubts, fears, and many things they do not do well; yet, when you are feeling low, you might forget this. Comparing yourself to others at this stage will likely only make you feel worse about yourself, so avoid it as much as possible.

I remember hearing Oprah say, "I never feel how they look." She is referring to how she feels when she sees celebrities on the red carpet. She is basically saying, *I never feel on the inside how they look on the outside.*

Take heart in knowing that everyone - even seemingly larger than life figures - can feel imposter syndrome too.

> **Pro Tip**: *Never compare your day-to-day to someone else's highlight reel.*

Here is another great example. This award-winning author, Neil Gaiman, will never forget the time he felt like he wasn't good enough.

"...Some years ago, I was lucky enough to be invited to a gathering of great and good people: artists and scientists, writers and discoverers of things. And I felt at any moment they would realize that I didn't qualify to be there, among these people who had really done things.

On my second or third night there, I was standing at the back of the hall, while musical entertainment happened, and I started talking to a very nice, polite, elderly gentleman about several things, including our shared first name. And then he pointed to the hall of people, and said words to the effect of, 'I just look at all these people, and I think, what the heck am I doing here? They've made amazing things. I just went where I was sent.'

And I said, 'Yes. But you were the first man on the moon. I think that counts for something.'"

Neil Gaiman was talking to Neil Armstrong.

Run your race. Remember the progress you have made and focus on the progress you are making (and will continue to make if you choose to not give up).

Take the Smallest Win

Sometimes, when we are looking at an instance of failure, the whole event en masse seems overwhelming. It feels like a vast, nebulous, monolithic thing that's *all* bad. However, there are probably quite a few takeaways you can feel good about and build on next time.

The next time you are beating yourself up over a past failure, be sure to scan through and look for the small wins in the situation. You may have to look harder and longer in some situations than in others, but you will find them.

Story: *When I was in grade school, I had bombed a math test. Math was my least favorite subject, and long division was a beast. I returned home after getting my test results back. My teacher had drenched the double-sided piece of paper in red ink from top to bottom. The ink bled through the paper as if it were a Rorschach test, the red marks on both sides were that prominent. I had only gotten three questions out of twenty right. I was embarrassed and didn't want to tell my mom and dad.*

My older brother was home visiting from college at the time. He noticed I was a bit down and asked me what was up. I told him I failed my math test. He said, "Let me see it." I gave it to him, watching closely for his reaction. I knew that there was nothing good on that paper, and this was just going to be one of those heart-to-heart conversations where he said, "Yep, this is pretty bad."

He carefully looked over each side of the paper. He probably knew his reaction and what he said in the next 5-10 seconds could crush his baby sister. He was looking at the test for the longest time, until he finally looked at me. He then said, "Well...it's...clear you understand the concept of division from the three you got right, so that's good. If you just build on that with the bigger numbers, you'll be good."

I only got those three questions right because all I had to do was divide the number by 1. It's the most straightforward division problem. However, I did get them right. And it proved, kind of, that I at least knew what division was. It was no doubt a small win, but I still took it.

If you're having a hard time seeing the good in a certain situation, it may be useful to seek an objective, outside opinion from someone you trust.

> **Quote:** *"I succeed because I'm willing to fail more times than you will try."*
>
> *- Anonymous*

Step Up to The Next Level

Getting ready to loop back up and go to the next level may require something new or different from you. It's the "what got you here won't get you there" sentiment. I've heard many people described this stage as the point where your actual self meets your aspirational self. The concept being, you're at the edge of your current capabilities. Now, you must take the next step. Step into your *aspirational self-* into your best version of yourself that's a little further ahead than where you are now.

Imagine yourself standing right in front of a hologram that looks just like you. You can see a hazy outline of what could be, and you can almost touch it. In order to become this version of you, all you have to do is you step into it, inhabit it and become it.

Another way to think of it is like a snake shedding its old skin. When the old skin has served its purpose, it sheds in order to make room for something new and fresh.

Another way to think of it, is to compare it to the alchemy of metal. Picture a container of hot metal with a sifter circulating and rotating through it; this is the purification process - it separates the highest quality elements from the rest.

Keep working on this part of the process repeatedly. Always continue to rejuvenate, reinvent, and refine yourself. Doing so will keep you at the top of your game.

> **Quote:** *"Without being willing to fail and continually get back up again, I would have never been able to find the right market and establish my product within it."*
>
> *- Kelly Manthey, Group Chief Executive at Kin+Carta*

> **Pro Tip:** *A good exercise you can practice to make sure you are on the right path is to think back at an event that used to scare you, one that was such a big deal awhile back. Then ask yourself if you still feel the same way about it now. If the answer is yes, then try to figure out why.*
>
> *If the answer is no, then take a moment to acknowledge your growth and give yourself some much deserved credit.*

Decision vs. Outcome

An important lesson to learn in order to be successful, is to separate the decision from the outcome. People often conflate how good of a decision-maker someone is based on the *outcome* of this person's choices. I feel I need to emphasize this principle because I get a lot of push back on this one: the initial decision about something and the ultimate result can be two completely separate entities.

It's easy to say things like, "I shouldn't have taken this job, look at how it turned out." Or, "Why did I take the shortcut to work? If I hadn't, then I wouldn't have gotten in this accident." But if you flip the outcome, the decision may all of a sudden appear like a stroke of genius.

You could instead say, "Taking this new job was a risk, but it's one of the best decisions I've made; it was a springboard for my career." Or, "I was so glad I remembered the shortcut, I made up for the lost time and got to the meeting right on time."

Hindsight bias is a beautiful thing. We can all sit there and say, "Knowing what I know now, of course, I should have done this thing or that." A more helpful approach is to look back and ask: "Was that the very best decision I could have made at the time with all the information I had?"

If the answer is yes, then rest easy. If it was the very best you could have done, then by definition, you could not have done any more.

If the answer is no, *even at the time* you knew in your heart of hearts that it wasn't the best decision, reflect on it and then throw it in the feedback loop. Learn from your mistakes and use it as fuel to do better the next time.

A great book on decision vs. outcome is *Thinking In Bets* by Annie Duke. In one example, she cites a play call made by Pete Carroll. He was the head coach of the Seattle Seahawks football team at the end of Superbowl 49. With seconds remaining, the Seahawks were on the 1-yard line which meant they were only 1 yard away from scoring a touchdown that would result in their victory. Everyone thought it would be a running play. The quarterback, Russell Wilson, would hand the ball off to running back Marshawn Lynch (who was one of the best in the game). Instead, it was a pass play. A New England Patriot intercepted the pass; the Patriots won the game.

In her book, the author breaks down why the decision to pass the ball was the best one to make at the time - statistically speaking, since it had the highest chance of success.

Pete Carroll was slaughtered in the press for weeks after the game ended. During an interview, one reporter told Pete that the play call was one of "...the worst [play] call you made." Pete politely corrected the reporter and said, "Well, it was one of the worst outcomes, yes." He then goes on to mention that if the other team had not intercepted the pass, then the Seahawks would have won. If that outcome had happened, then the press would have been singing a different tune. He went on to say that he takes 100% responsibility for the call and outlined why he had decided to do what he did at the time. Pete is a great coach and a great leader.

Make the best decision you can with all the information you have at the time.

> **Pro Tip**: Don't look at a decision in terms of "right" or "wrong." Try not to put so much pressure on yourself by thinking, I'm either going to make the right decision or wrong decision.
> Look at it as Choice A and Choice B; neither one is better than the other. They both have pros and cons and their own set of trade-offs.

Fuel the Liftoff

After a "failure event," you may need to let things settle for a bit; let time do its thing. This interval can be seconds, minutes, days, or weeks depending on how you feel about it. Then, you're looking up at the last leg of the loop to get yourself back up to forward progress. It's the steepest part to climb and sometimes, requires an additional boost. That extra bit of fuel comes from using all the components we've covered thus far to push you forward.

Remember, you are doing what others can't or won't. Take pride in the fact you are doing the work. *These moments* - not waving from a podium - is where champions are made. Take the lesson and the learning and then keep your eyes fixed forward. *Look in the direction you want to go.*

> **Pro Tip:** Like a car, you have a tiny rearview mirror and a great big windshield. Where you are going is more important than what is behind you.

Remember, this so-called failure is temporary. Don't dwell in it. Don't set up camp. Don't drown in pools of pessimism. This is a pit stop. Re-tool, re-fuel, and be on your way.

As you become better and better at navigating the loop, you'll start to feel more confident. Once you start to gain confidence, then the loops will become shorter and you will move back up quicker. You may *even* look forward to your next loop. It's a sign that you're growing, improving, progressing, and moving in the right direction.

And, if you get really good, then you can even learn to use it as part of a Swizzle... we will talk about that more in the next chapter.

Key Takeaways:

- Life will give you a swift kick in the pants sometimes. So learn how to get better at looping up.
- Be aware of where you are in the process and what strategies or tools will help you in that stage.
- Find the lesson or takeaway in each failure and use it as fuel to move forward. Transform failure to progress.

Key Questions:

- What would you do today if you knew you couldn't fail?
- What will let you know you're at the bottom of the loop?
- What go-to strategies or tools will you use to loop up?

CHAPTER 2

SWIZZLE

"Absorb what is useful. Discard what is not. Add what is uniquely your own."

- Bruce Lee

The first time I would say this word, I'd usually get a slight head tilt with furrowed, quizzical eyebrows. The listener is amused and curious. It sounds a little funny. By context, and the fact the word sounds like its meaning, they get what I'm saying. Eventually, people around me start using it themselves: my teams, my colleagues, and my clients. I've heard it modified to "Swizz," Swizzalege," and "for the Swizzle." I have even heard it used at a board meeting. Every time I hear it, it brings a smile to my face.

Swizzle Definition

Swizzle   (SWIZZ-uhl)

Verb: To take the best components of several different items or areas and combine them to make new and better materials. Uniquely applied to a situation by an individual.

Okay, so maybe it doesn't look like a word that should belong in a book called *Hacking Executive Leadership; however,* executive thinking is out-of-the-box thinking. It's multi-faceted and draws on all areas and aspects of you and your life in order to creatively problem-solve. It's the penultimate of resourcefulness.

It's essential to pay attention to the overall framework you're using to be the most influential leader. The framework you have now affects everything you do and how you operate in the world. The mindset and filter you have in place guides how you gather, structure and seek out certain types of information.

As an executive, you're limiting yourself if you have a narrow, old or faulty framework. Swizzling allows for a more holistic approach. You become the conduit and catalyst for taking in multiple sources of information and in turn, you are absorbing and transforming them into useful materials for yourself and those around you.

Tap into your full potential. Expand the resources, learnings, insights and "Aha!" moments available to you.

Let's jump into some examples.

Adaptability Swizzle

Floyd Mayweather

I listen to podcasts all the time. I'll often plug in my AirPods and listen to them in the background as I do other activities. I travel frequently, so I consume a lot of information in cars, on planes, walking through airports, and standing in security lines.

In one podcast, Floyd Mayweather, the champion boxer, was being interviewed. All I know about boxing is relegated to the *Rocky* movies. If I ever need to train for a boxing match, I'm pretty sure I'd need to run in slow motion on a beach and beat Apollo Creed to know if I'm ready.

The host asked Mayweather several questions about his training. He kept trying to get Mayweather to describe why he was so good. He wanted to know why he was such a skilled athlete. Was it just a natural physical talent? Was that why his hands were so quick and why his footwork was so impressive? After a while, Mayweather finally answered. He admitted that his adaptability was what made him so deadly as a boxer. His *adaptability*-not his hands, not his footwork, not anything else to do with his physical prowess. He said no opponent is the same, no two rounds are the same, and it was his ability to adapt on the fly that made him a winner. He was better at *that* than anybody else.

I was listening to this podcast while I was driving, and I knew right away that it was a concept that could be applied to many areas of life. I would keep it and store it away in my mental toolbox. I would later pull it out and apply it in any situation that I see fit. In business, unexpected events happen all the time - whether it be an issue with a client account, a personnel matter that needs attention, or technological malfunctioning. In health and fitness, you can learn to be adaptable as well. You can meal prep in advance and leave some meals in a communal fridge at the office at the beginning of the week. That way, on the days you end up needing to stay late, you can adjust to your busy schedule without giving up your diet plans. Even if your simple weekend to-do list is foiled by something you hadn't planned for, you can still try to be as productive as possible. Learning how to be adaptable is not easy but it is a great skill to have. Once you have honed in on being adaptable, then you will realize how much easier things will start to feel for you.

General Stanley McChrystal

I was listening to another podcast with General Stanley McChrystal. McCrystal was in command of Joint Special Operations in the mid-2000s. His last assignment was commanding forces in Afghanistan. In one segment of the podcast, he explained that in his line of work, things around you are continually changing. This means that you have to be consistently good at changing as well. "Every situation is so unique...even for a leader to be a leader on Monday and try the same things on Tuesday is a loser," he said, "Your consistency is your ability to adapt."

There was that word again, adapt. How consistent was my adaptability? Was I adapting appropriately to the various meetings I had throughout the week? Was I conveying the relevant information to the team meetings on Monday and Tuesday? Was I showing up with the energy I wanted to for each? Maybe something was more suited to the specific audience or topic I was covering. Has anything significant in the business changed between Monday and Tuesday that I need to cover?

When I heard this quality described a second time, I knew it was something very important. Two people at the top of their fields said this skill is vital. What is interesting is the fact that these two people belong to two very different fields-boxing and military generalship. Yet, they both agree that adaptability is a needed skill. It is important to pay attention to patterns you see over and over again, especially if these patterns seem to span across different fields. The fact that they work for so many people means that they are universal skills which means they are skills that you would do well to invest in.

Make It All Your Own

Swizzling does not involve *impersonating* anyone else. In the cases above, I'm certainly not trying to be Floyd Mayweather or Stanley McCrystal. I've taken their advice, but I've also put my personal spin on it. Sometimes, it's even taking the *spirit of the* topic being discussed. I simply take what works for me and leave the rest.

What might be "good" and works well for one person may not work for you, and that's perfectly fine. Something that has helped them may not be suited for you or be applicable to your situation for a myriad of reasons. It may not work well for your personality, temperament, particular circumstance - or maybe it will not work for you *right now*. However, it might be useful in five weeks or even five years.

Realizing this doesn't mean you can't admire the trait or skill in the other person. On the contrary, if they've found something that works for them and are rockin' it, celebrate and cheer them on. Be confident and know that you will find your unique strengths and you will also know the right way to apply and express those strengths as well.

Essentialism Swizzle

The book *Essentialism* by Greg McKeown is one of the top 10 books I'd recommend for leaders (and for anyone really) to read. This book deals with identifying and placing a laser focus on the crucial things in your life. It teaches you how to determine what is essential and how to discard distractions. It is so much more than a time management book; it is a mindset, almost a philosophy. It teaches you how to dedicate your time and energy towards your highest contribution. One of the main principles in the book is focusing on *one* thing and doing it well versus trying to do a dozen things mediocrely. I've recreated a graphic from the book below:

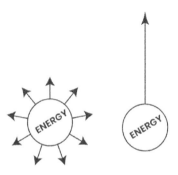

What is truly essential? Focus and prioritize to get further, faster.

I love this principle. The notion of wanting and trying to do so many things at once resonated with me. In my 20s, I had a myriad of hobbies. There was weight training, piano lessons, Arabic lessons, financial investing, ballroom dance lessons (sadly *Dancing with the Stars* did not call), etc. There were several points in time where I was juggling half a dozen different things throughout the month. Being involved in so many different activities was great at the time. I got to explore different interests, was exposed to different groups of people, and was able to figure out what I liked and what I didn't.

In my 30s, I got a better sense of what I wanted to do and what projects and skills came more naturally to me. I then decided to narrow down the number of hobbies I was pursuing. I only gave my time and energy to the hobbies that I was especially interested in and wanted to get better at.

I took what applied to me in the book and swizzled it for my situation. Instead of choosing just one interest as my main hobby, I narrowed it down to three. The concept of Essentialism still holds true however. I was able to go further, faster with the three hobbies versus six plus. I could have narrowed it down to one, but having just one hobby didn't suit me. I liked to have some variety. I'll also cycle through my top three - putting a little more time and focus on one hobby and less on the other two, then I'll rotate. This approach works very well for me now, so I will keep doing it. In the future, if something else suits me better, then I will have no problem changing it up again.

Feedback Swizzle

A Toastmasters group is a gathering where people meet and practice their public speaking skills. Typically, a group will meet weekly, and one or two people will give a prepared speech to the group. Two other people are designated as "evaluators" and it is their role to provide feedback on the speaker's speech. Feedback can include emphasis on volume, vocal variety, pacing, use of hand gestures, and body language. Receiving feedback, of course, helps the speaker get better. One of the central tenets of Toastmasters is providing a safe, supportive, and encouraging space for people to practice. This principle is especially important for evaluators to keep in mind when giving their feedback.

I remember there was one gentleman in my Toastmasters group years ago who was an *excellent* evaluator. I perked up and paid attention anytime he was evaluating a speech.

The structure of his feedback usually consisted of three main parts.

First, he would open with something he liked or thought the speaker did well. He would not only say it, but he would also include a specific example.

Second, he would bring up something the speaker could improve upon. He would also give a specific example. He would often use phrases like:

> *"An idea for your next speech..."*
>
> *"One option to make that transition bit smoother could be..."*
>
> *"If you want to build on what you did there, you can..."*

"Also, just to bring to your awareness, many speakers don't even know they do this when they…"

Third, he described something the speaker did well. He once again gave a specific example. Here, he would save the best for last. He would have a big smile on his face and would gesture with not only his hands but with his whole body. He was genuinely excited for the speaker. He would say things like:

"The best thing you did…."

"My absolute favorite thing that happened during the speech…"

"I really want to congratulate you on…"

"Remember X. That was very strong and stood out. I'd definitely incorporate that into your future presentations if you can. Great job, there."

This structure was useful because it not only gave the speaker valuable information, but it was delivered effectively as well. The first section was upbeat and eased the speaker in. It avoided smacking them over the head with what they did "wrong" right out of the gate. This is important since the speaker was probably still very nervous after giving his/her speech to the whole group. The second section, which can be seen as the most valuable part of the evaluator's comments, gave the speaker something to improve on. The third section left them on a high note, with a kind compliment.

The use of specific examples throughout was incredibly helpful as well because the speaker knew precisely what the evaluator was referring to. This saves the speaker from having to wonder what part of the speech the evaluator was referring to. A comment like, "Your opening was great!" is nice but it could leave the speaker confused. Which part of the opening was the evaluator referring to?

This evaluator would also vary the comments he made based on two main factors: the speaker's level and the speaker's individual personality.

If he was evaluating a member who had been speaking for ten years in the club and was very advanced, then he would comment on more advanced techniques. For instance, suggesting a small difference in hand gesture during a particular line, a specific word choice during a transition between sections, or using a dropping versus rising voice inflection at a pivotal moment.

For beginners, he knew a much different approach was needed. Sometimes, if a brand-new member just stood there and read their first speech word-for-word without passing out, that was a win for them. He would never comment on their lack of hand gestures or nitpick their word choice in these cases. Instead, he'd focus on congratulating them for completing their first Toastmasters speech - what an achievement!

He also tailored his approach to the individual speaker and how they'd received information. Some speakers needed sugar-coating. They needed the evaluator to ham up the positives so they did not crumble into pieces. Some speakers preferred direct communication in an almost challenging, "I bet you can do better" kind of way. The evaluator switched up his content and delivery accordingly. Sometimes he would add more "good" examples and be more effusive with his praise. Other times, he would downplay any superfluous comments and get straight to what could be improved—even adding two or three examples of how they could improve for next time.

I've used this framework many, many times in business. From giving formal feedback to my direct reports on performance reviews, to more casual feedback for a colleague on a dry-run of their presentation. I keep in mind if this person is a "beginner" or "advanced" at a skill and where this person is in his/her career. I also consider how the speaker would like to receive information and try to cater to that.

To swizzle it further, one tweak I'll make is asking a *question*. In Toastmasters, the structure and time-limit for the evaluators' comments don't allow for this. However, in real-world business interactions, asking the other person's opinion and making feedback sessions more of a conversation can be valuable. There will be more on communication, delivering feedback, and asking powerful questions in later chapters.

Boss Swizzle

As an executive, you most likely have multiple teams, layers of people, and managers rolling up to you. We've all had bosses. Hopefully, you've been fortunate enough to have some great people you have loved working for, ones that you learned from and respected. You've also probably had less than stellar bosses whose "leadership" style is cringeworthy and dealing with them was stress-inducing.

Since you are now the boss, that means that many people will look up to you to see what kind of leader you are. Craft and infuse your leadership style with what is useful, stay away from what was not successful, and remember to make it all your own.

Take a previous boss of mine, we'll call her Amanda. Amanda was a Silicon Valley-type entrepreneur. She didn't come from money, and she was making it on her own. She took a big risk, and started a company from nothing. The business was successful, and it was her baby. She ate, slept, and drank it 24/7/365 - even bragging that she had taken work calls on her wedding day.

I learned a tremendous amount from Amanda about how to run a start-up business from the ground up. When I think of Amanda or whenever I am asked to describe her, there is one word that always comes to mind: relentless.

Amanda was the epitome of relentless- in all the negative and positive connotations of the word. She was a perfectionist and wanted things just so. She would argue for hours with our CTO over the design and style of a single button. She would listen to a client call through the walls, and then would barge in and just start talking. She also had this odd quirk about her. She would beeline from her office to the printer and then start to furiously spray the printer with an air canister cleaner. The first time this happened, I thought there must have been a very important print job coming. After this happened several times and nothing ever printed, I realized it was just her compulsion to make sure the printer was pristine.

On the flip side, she was available whenever you needed her. She was "on" all the time even if she didn't feel like it. I remember one morning, I saw her walking in. There was something important in an email that I had sent her. It was top of mind and a big deal for me, and I wanted to get it resolved as soon as possible. However, I knew it wasn't the most critical thing in the company and I decided to wait until later to talk to Amanda about it.

When she walked in, she looked exhausted. You could tell she hadn't gotten any sleep and was gutting through it. Still, without pausing, she walked in from the front door directly to my office, not even stopping to put her bag down. She calmly sat down and said, "I can go over that email with you now." I looked a little surprised and said, "Amanda, if you want to grab a cup of coffee and get settled in or something, that's no problem." Without missing a beat, she said, "Nope, I'm here," with a soft smile. And she was "here," -she was engaged and sharp and "on it." Like always.

I remember how that made me feel, and now I can better identify and step into certain leadership moments with Amanda's "on" spirit in mind. When something doesn't seem like a big deal to me, but it is being brought to my attention by someone on my team, I can do a quick mental check on what this means to him/her. When something critical hits my inbox first thing in the morning, it's game time. Even if the coffee hasn't seeped in yet, I can step up when I need to. I still take on a little bit of Amanda's spirit and approach. I will continue to use it to my advantage in order to benefit my teams.

Amanda was also a very matter of fact person. She was edgy and was not worried about being politically correct. In most situations, Amanda didn't care about hurting people's feelings. She could behave this way as it was her company and she ran the show. On one occasion, she became very upset when a team member made a mistake. This outburst was in a main area of the office with low cubicles where everyone could see and hear. Shortly after, she was shown a data point that proved there, in fact, was not a mistake. She immediately and calmly said, "Oh, I'm sorry, I see now." She then turned and put her hand on the shoulder of the team member and even more calmly, said, "I'm sorry about that, Matt." The delivery was still not overly-effusive, but it was genuine and diffused the situation.

I remember watching Amanda at that moment and knowing her response to that situation was an element of leadership I wanted to be able to emulate. Now, I have a blueprint for calmly admitting when you're wrong on the spot. While I still don't like the moment I realize I'm wrong, I know it doesn't need to be a huge song and dance of feeling guilty, then embarrassed, then having the emotions get high, then letting them cool off, and finally, asking for "forgiveness." It was better to just do it right there in the moment. However, it was important to be genuine. Once I have apologized and the other person has accepted, then we can both move on. Everyone is okay, and it saves time and mental energy.

Take what is useful.

Being relentless in a good way and being on point when your team needs you.

Discard what is not.

Don't listen through walls, it's creepy and awkward; I'm also fine with the health standard accepted levels of cleanliness for office equipment.

Make it all your own.

Don't try to impersonate your old boss, take elements of their leadership that worked well and lace it in with your style.

Weight Training Swizzle

In weight training, there is a theory created and described by Dr. Mike Israetel and Dr. James Hoffman of Renaissance Periodization around volume landmarks. This model outlines how much weight you should lift and what number of repetitions you should do to gain the most muscle. For example, if you have leg day and are doing squats, what combination of pounds on the bar and repetitions should you use and complete? If you're into weight training, I'd highly recommend checking out the full explanation. Here is a very high-level summary of three prominent landmarks for this example:

- **MV = Maintenance Volume**
    - "This is the amount of training...that allows you to maintain your current level of muscular size."

- **MAV = Maximum Adaptive Volume**
    - "...the range of volumes in which you make your best gains."

- **MRV = Maximum Recoverable Volume**
    - "Your body can only recover from so much. Once all of your body's recovery systems are in full use, any more disruption to the system [training] will cause incomplete recovery during that time."

So, what is the optimal volume to gain muscle? It's a range. The range between Maximum Adaptable Volume and Maximum Recoverable Volume. *However*, pay attention to the Maximum Recoverable Volume landmark. If you go over this, you are *exceeding* the amount of volume from which your body can recover. In other words, at some point, you have to rest. To be the most effective and efficient at gaining muscle, you must pay attention to your recovery. It is equally important as the intensity of your workout.

When you are in the gym lifting weights, one way you grow muscle is by breaking down muscle - the overload is causing microtears. During recovery, your body is healing those tears and making them a little bit stronger in the process. Once you properly recover, you come back again and perform better and make even more gains.

This means there is not a linear progression. You can't just keep lifting more and more weight or doing more and more repetitions. After a certain point, it's counterproductive. At best, it's just wasting time and energy ("junk volume"). At worst, it can actually hurt you (you can injure yourself).

Lift and shift this concept to business. When you're at the office, staying late to work on a project, there is a point of diminishing returns. This tipping point is when it's not worth working longer hours. This is because the quality of work is suffering and you are not going to make any meaningful "gains." It would be better to leave, rest up, and come back fresh. You can think of this concept in the time frame of a single day or an extended period of time. Maybe you can go hard for a few weeks or even months, but eventually, you need to build in the recovery time to be at your best.

Know where your volume landmarks are. Keep your target range in mind so you can stay at peak performance in the long run.

> **Pro Tip:** *Remember, your target range is not static. It will move, evolve, ebb, and flow. An effective work session for the healthy, well-rested version of you may be different for the not as healthy, not as a well-rested version. Be attuned to where you and adjust accordingly.*

Grant Cardone + the Meditation Swizzle

As you take swizzling to heart, you'll start seeing new patterns pop up like John Nash seeing numbers light up and come out of the wall in *A Beautiful Mind*. As you do this, make sure you apply the appropriate dose of it to any given situation.

Grant Cardone

Take Grant Cardone, for instance. He's gregarious, loud and has a larger-than-life personality - you can watch five minutes of him on YouTube to get what I mean. If you buy his book

The 10X Rule, I'd highly recommend the audio version because he reads it himself, and you can feel the energy. He takes the "go-big-or-go-home-supersize-your-goals-don't-care-about-what-anyone-else-says-or-thinks-get-after-it-today" approach.

Sometimes, his persona is a bit too much for me. I'd have to set him aside for a while. Yet, there are other times when I absolutely love his all-out, "burn the boats" mentality. It's just what I need. I keep his book downloaded on Audible. If I'm going into a big meeting or I hit a rut with a project I'm working on, I'll listen to a few minutes of his book. It's like a shot glass of motivation.

Now, would I swizzle the essence of Grant Cardone and get fired up right before I'm about to speak to someone about the funeral arrangements for their grandpa? *No.* This would not be the appropriate time or place for that. Please, swizzle responsibly.

+ Meditation

I know meditation is good for you. Many, many people have been doing it for thousands of years with positive results. However, if I'm coaching a high-powered executive or entrepreneur who runs a million miles a minute, talks fast, thinks fast, moves fast, and is all about the productivity of every minute, am I going to recommend sitting still and meditating for two hours a day? Hell no. Even if being Buddha on the mountain would benefit them and everyone around them. They'd probably look at me with shock and horror or just a blank stare of utter incomprehension.

In this scenario, I'd need to meet them where they're at. If being more present or mindful is something they are trying to get better at and want to explore meditating as a possible avenue, then it may be easier to start them off with meditating one minute a day.

Or it could be batching it with another activity or event that they already have built in. When you brush your teeth, take that minute or two to be aware of the room you're in. When you walk through a certain doorway, take a full deep breath. When your Fitbit or Apple Watch buzzes with a notification, pick a sense to pay attention to (i.e., take a few seconds to notice what you're hearing, what surface you're sitting or standing on, look at three objects in your view and really see and notice them, etc.). Another great one is a walking meditation - this allows a person to move around instead of sitting still and it usually gets them outside for some fresh air.

Story: *I personally like to take walks. They are not "walking meditations" per se. But I try not to take my phone with me to limit distractions. Several years ago, I was riding an elevator down to take one of these walks. An elderly gentleman who looked to be in his 80s got in.*

He looked me up and down - his face starting with concern and confusion and ending with a smile and chuckle. He then said, "You...you don't have a phone. That's amazing. I've never seen one of you, youngsters, without one...that's just something to see these days."

Small Swizzles

There are smaller, more tactical swizzles to keep in mind as well.

A small swizzle can be as simple as one line in an email. A salesperson at a company I used to work with would use the phrase, "Thank you for any info or assistance!" at the end of his emails when asking a question. I liked it. I thought it was a nice way of acknowledging I was helping him out with something and thanking me for it. So now, I use it when applicable.

A small swizzle can be a small habit. An old boss I had early in my career used to walk into the room where our team sat, which was quite far from her office and say good morning with a smile and a nod. She did it every morning. It was a very short exchange, but it was something nice that I still remember. I've used that when I've had teams with similar logistics.

A small swizzle can be prepping a PowerPoint presentation. Have a quarterly all-company meeting coming up and need to get your segment of slides ready to go? Take some slides from the last three months' business review decks you already have and some slides from your team meeting you did last week and swizzle them. Put the relevant slides together in a new deck, make the formatting consistent, flip through the slides to make sure everything flows together and, voila!

Anti-Swizzles

Keep your radar up for "anti-swizzles," too. These can be for larger and smaller scale items.

If there are qualities and characteristics you repeatedly see - with different people, in various fields - that seem to be a universal detriment or downfall, take note. Try to avoid, eliminate, or minimize them as much as possible.

Hone your leadership by paying attention to what *not* to do as well.

Be on the Lookout (for Swizzles)!

If you take nothing else away from this chapter, remember to *actively* look for opportunities to swizzle.

Setting this intention is like telling your brain to look for red cars. You'll start seeing them everywhere, even though there is the same amount as before.

You probably have at least a handful of "new" things you can apply right now. Think about what you know, places you've been, people you've met, something you've heard or read, experiences you've had.

Going forward, you now have an expanded pool of resources to draw on. This reservoir can include your boss, your colleagues, a friend, a leader you don't know but admire, a podcast, an interaction at the grocery store, an observation in an airport, an advertisement, and so on and so forth. Optimize your experiences and use them to your advantage.

Another great thing about swizzling is that the model grows and evolves with you. As you go through life, what you swizzle - what you notice, interpret and bring in - will grow and mature as well.

Take the example of wanting to have fun. What is fun at 14 years old is different than at 24 and then 34. The same holds true for goals such as always wanting to learn and improve, treating people with respect, and being an effective problem-solver. What those things mean to you and how you go about doing them will change. This change might be a function of time - you'll give a different meaning to all these things at different stages of your life. It might be through an experience - when you actually experience something yourself (it's no longer theoretical or something that happens to "other people"), it may change your perspective.

Through it all, you can continuously be on the lookout. Be curious and excited about what might present itself. Swizzling will serve you well.

Key Takeaways:

- The framework itself is essential; pay attention to which one you're using.
- What you swizzle and how you swizzle will be unique to you; make it your own.
- Actively look for opportunities to swizzle; be open and creative to learning and applying new ideas.

Key Questions:

- What areas can you leverage for swizzling?
- What will you do to apply them in your own way?
- Are there any themes or patterns you have seen come up across different areas?

CHAPTER 3

CONTACT LENS

"...we are not all watching the same movie. Even if we all find ourselves in the exact same situation, based on our individual Styles we will tend to experience moments very differently from one to another."

- Stan Phelps, et al., Diamond Goldfish: Excel Under Pressure & Thrive in the Game of Business

We all have a set of beliefs that shape our world. Everything we see, hear, and experience is taken in through this lens. It's like a contact lens. Once you put a pair in, everything you see filters through it. If those contact lenses were tinted yellow, everything you looked at would have a sheen of yellow. If you switched them to blue, now everything would look blue-ish.

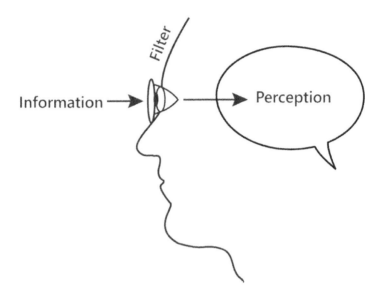

Everything you take in is filtered through whatever lens you have on.

In the real world, an eye doctor puts your eyes through a series of tests and comes up with a specific prescription that will help your eyes see the best. In our analogy, lenses are beliefs. These can be wide-ranging:

"The world is a friendly and favorable place."

"The world is scary and dangerous."

"Trust people until they prove otherwise."

"Don't trust anyone until they've earned it."

"Success equals how much someone is willing to pay you and what title you have."

"Success is peace of mind and freedom in my schedule."

"You can't be an involved, attentive parent and have an executive role."

"I can be very good at my C-Level position and not be overly stressed."

"I'm bad at public speaking."

"I'm getting better at public speaking every day."

All of these statements are beliefs, and they don't come close to an exhaustive list. If you think about any two people in the world, they will have a different lens and the way they see the world will also differ.

Another characteristic of contact lenses is that they are very close to you. Physically, they are right on your eyeball. This placement is by design, and of course, has its advantages. You don't have anything on your face, which some people like for practical or aesthetic purposes. The placement of the lens also means you can *easily forget that they are on.*

In the same way, you can be "wearing" beliefs for years and forget they are on. *Or* you may not even be aware you have them on at all. This would be like someone putting contact lenses on you as a baby or small child and you not knowing there could be another way of seeing things. These are called hidden beliefs - or blind spots - and everyone has them.

A large part of being an effective leader is "knowing thyself." Becoming aware of your blind spots is a crucial step. Hidden beliefs are a big chunk of your operating system. They are running, automatically, every minute of every day. You should make sure you have a vote on what they are.

You are the vehicle or mechanism or instrument through which you lead. Make sure you are aware of the main components of your internal system. To give one practical example, you are one half of the equation in every conversation. Having a sense of how you tend to receive and interpret data - and what assumptions or biases you have built-in - will help you think and act with more clarity.

Question your current belief set. Take inventory. Make sure the lenses you have on are serving you well.

Hidden Beliefs

There are a multitude of factors that go into creating your unique belief set. Childhood is a big one, of course - when you grew up, where you grew up, your parents, what sort of environment you were in, etc. Other broad influences can be religion, education, major life events, friends, and people with whom you spend the most time. As a small child, you inherit the beliefs of the adults around you.

However, a belief may serve you well in one phase of life and not make sense to hold onto in another. For example, small children are often told, "Don't talk to strangers." This advice is perfectly sound if little Billy is about to walk to school by himself for the first time. The same direction would seem a bit odd and misplaced if you were talking to Billy as an adult going into a networking function for work.

There's a group of beliefs that tag along from childhood to adulthood that you don't consciously know about or choose to have. These are your hidden beliefs.

Now wait a minute, you might reply, "Are you saying I believe things I don't know about? That's pretty far-fetched." Let's use the example of language. If you are reading or listening to this book, that means you have learned a language. For most children, the first language they learn to speak is determined by where they grew up and who their parents are. Language is a system and set of rules ingrained in you from a young age. Now, you use them daily without conscious thought.

For English speakers, the noun automatically comes before the verb; you know how to conjugate the past, future, and present tense. Determining the proper conjugation is done with ease, even with the special rules for irregular verbs.

Now, *when was the last time you consciously thought,* "John bounced the ball" was correct over "Bounced the ball John"?

How about knowing that it's "Jane went to the store," and not "Jane go-ed to the store"?

For native speakers, you don't *think* about it. You just do it. You have the "belief" of the English language. Hidden beliefs can be carried into adulthood with the same lack of thought or choice. They are grandfathered in, literally.

Better 1 or Better 2?

Now that you know the power of beliefs, you might be asking, "Okay, how do I identify which ones I have now (especially if they're hidden)?"

One of the best ways is by engaging with a professional coach. If you have a trusted mentor or friend, then they might be helpful resources to use as well. An objective, outside opinion is beneficial.

You *can* do a bit of self-coaching. If you're going to do this yourself, the best way is to reverse engineer this sequence:

BELIEFS → FEELINGS → ACTIONS

It all starts with what you believe.

What we believe about a situation will make us feel a certain way about the outcome. How we feel leads to how we behave and act. While the root belief is hidden, what you do and how you feel are clues. How you feel is more easily described. For instance, most of the time, you'd be able to tell me how you felt in a certain situation. What you do is observable - from yourself and other people - you could tell me that you raised your voice and shouted at Nancy in the meeting. Nancy could tell me that too.

Think of a recent event or exchange and ask yourself:

1. What was the action or behavior?
2. What was the feeling that prompted that?

With these data points, try to pinpoint the belief(s) generating and bringing up that feeling. At this point, you may need to do some detective work. Here are some sample questions that may help:

1. Why am I feeling that way? Why am I feeling *that* way? Asking why a couple of times can be like peeling back layers of an onion to get to the core idea.
2. What do I believe about that situation? That person? Myself in that scenario?
3. What am I *assuming*? Do you *know* something is true?
4. What's the difference between how I logically think about this and how I emotionally respond to it?
5. What is the opposing belief to the one I am thinking about?
6. Did this event remind me of a past event? It was just like when...

> **Pro Tip:** *Look for patterns. If you tend to feel or act a certain way in a specific situation, around a particular person, or whenever a topic comes up, then this can provide extra insight.*

A professional business or life coach is a fantastic resource here. They will provide an objective as well as an outside opinion. Not to mention they are also trained to ask helpful questions to uncover blind spots.

Just by having this new awareness and asking these questions, you'll be able to uncover some of your current wirings. Be vigilant and put your observer cap on throughout the next several days, weeks, months, and you will have more insights than ever before.

The next step, once you've identified your current beliefs, is *choosing* which set of lenses you want. You may choose to keep some beliefs from your past and set others down. You can decide to slightly alter some, and of course, add any new ones.

Coming up with your new set of lenses can be the fun part. You are in the driver's seat, and you get to decide how to shape your experience in the world. You see with a whole new set of eyes and look at everything from a new perspective. It can be a breath of fresh air.

This experience is like going to the eye doctor. Imagine your doctor placing the machine with two holes to see through against your face. Then your doctor will flip through a sequence of lenses and asks, "Any better one or better two?" "Are the letters clearer, brighter, bolder in 3 or 4?"

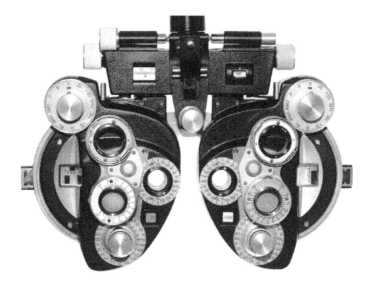

Write your own lens prescription.

Here are some key questions to ask when picking a new lens:

- What beliefs are serving me well?
- Is this belief helping or hindering me?
- How do I want to show up (in life in general or in certain situations)?
- Instead of feeling...about a person or topic, how do I want to feel about it?
- What would I need to *believe* in order to do that?

- What would the best version of myself do?
- What would someone I admire do?

You're looking for the aha moment, where you say, "Okay, yes, *if* I believed that, I would've shown up differently." The moment that thought pops up in your head, then you will know that you have found the new lens you want. Now that you have this new vision in mind, you know what lens you need to flip to. For some beliefs, this will be an easy switch. Once you know it, you can always go to it. Some will need constant reminders in order for them to become the new default lens. Stick with it and understand that each time you flip the lens, it will become easier.

Pro Tip: *Sometimes we become so familiar with a feeling - even if it's negative - that we might not want to change it. Without it, we can feel like we're in limbo or lost at sea. A common example is anxiety or stress.*

Most people would say they don't want to feel anxious or stressed. But if they've been used to feeling stressed for years and years and that has been their "go-to" feeling, it can be uncomfortable and unsettling to try and swap the belief that causes them to feel that way.

Keep this in mind: If you run into this, focus on the new, positive feelings and positive outcomes

> *you're opening up, and those beliefs will start to feel more familiar.*

One of my coaches uses a great technique with me by adding a modifier. When identifying and crafting a new belief, in the beginning, I might not believe it 100%. My coach will take me through identifying the action, feeling, belief sequence, and what I *want* that to look like. Then, narrowing down some potential new belief statements, she'll ask, "On a scale of 1-10, how much do you believe that?" It has to be a 10. It has to be that strong. If it's not, adding a modifier is a good step.

Here are some examples:

- I make good decisions. *Most of the time*, I make good decisions.
- I believe not having the answer is okay. *I'm learning to* believe that not having the answer is ok.
- Being mindful makes me more productive with higher quality results. Being mindful *helps* me be more productive with higher quality results.

I write these down and call them my "Belief 10s." I revisit the list and over time and I'm able to remove some modifiers.

Feel free to do this with some of your new belief statements and lenses.

> **Quote**: *"You are under no obligation to remain the same person you were a year ago, a moment ago, or even a day ago. You are here to create yourself, continuously."*
>
> *- Richard Feynman*

When you change your lens, you change your choices and actions. Your choices and actions determine your life trajectory. Make sure you have the right set in. Any better 1 or better 2?

You are Neo in The Matrix. At one point, you saw and experienced the world around you as it was presented to you by default lenses and beliefs. Now, you can observe it for what it is and deconstruct and manipulate its very makeup. *You can hack your beliefs.*

> **Quote**: Neo: What are you trying to tell me, that I can dodge bullets?
>
> Morpheus: No, Neo. I'm trying to tell you that when you're ready, you won't have to.
>
> - The Matrix

How to Frame Up Change

A universal topic is change. Everyone experiences changes in their lives. I've spoken to members of my teams, colleagues, clients, friends about this over the years. So, I want to take a quick moment to say a few words about it.

With an unexpected change or any sort of uncertainty, most people will automatically flip to a negative lens. New boss at work? Did the company announce a merger? A regulation shift in the industry? Time to get anxious, worried, and stressed. Time to flip to my "change is bad" lens.

- How does that make you feel?
- What action does it prompt you to take?
- How would you like to feel instead?
- What would be a more helpful action to take?

A different belief and a different lens would be "Change is neutral."

This lens is more helpful and more accurate. Change in and of itself isn't good or bad. It just is. The outcome of the change could be positive, negative, or just something new and different - not necessarily better or worse.

Don't believe me? If I told you, "Hey, you've just won 1 million dollars," that would be a change. How would you feel? What would you do? It would be a pretty positive response.

The next time a change comes up, remember to flip to the "Change is neutral" lens and be open to what will unfold and come of it.

> **Pro Tip:** *Often, a "setback" will become a setup for a new opportunity or a new chapter in your life. When it all comes together, you may even look back and see what you thought you wanted at the time would actually not have been the best path.*

Story: *A few years ago, my nephew was going through flight school to become a pilot and was about to graduate. It was time to apply for jobs. He wanted to go to Alaska and fly with one particular airline. He flew up to Alaska and found the office of the airline without having an interview setup. He didn't even rent a car, so he had to walk around to find the office. When he finally did, he couldn't find a way in or anyone to talk to. Just when he was about to give up, the hiring manager happened to come out of the door. He told her he had flown up here and walked around all day and would love to have a chance to speak with her briefly. She said yes, and they had a meeting.*

Several weeks later, he graduated from flight school. He was a certified pilot, which was a requirement for this airline. In the exchanges I had back and forth with him on his resume and cover letter, I asked where else he was applying. He said nowhere; he really wanted this one. I said I know you like this one, but what's your backup plan in case? He said he didn't have one because he only wanted to fly for this first airline.

He sent his resume and letter to the first airline. A few days passed and nothing. A few more days passed, and still nothing back. "It's okay," I told him, "You never know what's happening on their side not to make them write back - it could be hundreds of things that have nothing to do with you. If you don't get this one, a better one will come along." Not buying it at the time but he placated his aunt with a "Yeah, ok," as he kept waiting.

He never did hear back from the first airline. So, a few months later, my adventurous and determined nephew decided to move to Alaska without a job or place to stay. When he got there and was looking for a temporary job to bridge him through, a second airline contacted him. He interviewed with them and got the job! He was so excited. The position with the second airline had the types of airplanes he wanted to fly, and the routes and schedules suited him - it was a perfect fit.

While he was going through the second airline's training program, I came across a news article about the first airline. It had gone out of business. Had my nephew gotten the job with the first airline he had wanted, then he would have been out of a job. Not getting that first job was a blessing in disguise.

Key Takeaways:

- The lens you're looking through affects everything you see.

- Uncovering some of your hidden beliefs or blind spots makes you a more effective leader.
- You can switch out or flip to a new lens.

Key Questions:

- What lenses are you looking through now?
- Are they serving you well (or causing more harm than good)?
- What do you want your lenses and belief set to be going forward?

CHAPTER 4

PLAYBOOK

"It is what it is. But, it will be what you make it."

- Pat Summitt

N ow that you've become more aware of your current perspectives and are thinking about being *intentional* on what you want your framework and lens to be, let's build on that. It's time to put together your playbook.

Playbook Definition

In American football, the definition of a playbook is as follow:

> "A playbook is a collection of a football team's plays and strategies, all compiled and organized into one

book or binder. A team's playbook may be separated into sections for offensive plays, defensive plays and special teams, or they may have separate playbooks for each discipline."

A coach will develop a strategy and playbook for the team. Many teams have specific systems they use - a certain offensive design or a particular defensive style. The coach will recruit players with the skill sets and characteristics that work best in that system.

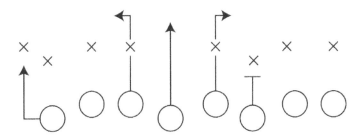

Create your own playbook.

When the coach calls a specific play from his playbook, it will be the one he thinks will give him and his team the best chance to accomplish their goal - for the offense, this is getting 10 yards down the field to earn a first down (which gives the offense four more tries to get 10 more yards). He will consider which specific play in this particular scenario will give his team the most significant advantage and highest likelihood.

You may have heard of a quarterback calling an "audible." The quarterback is the leader of the offense on the field. He is the one who gets the ball every play (to either pass or run). As he sets up at the line of scrimmage - the line where the offense and defense face each other before each down or set play - he will need to make an important decision. If he "reads" a specific type of defensive formation, then he will change the play call at the last minute. An audible is called when the quarterback doesn't think the original play call will work well or he thinks something else will work better. He will shout out the new play call to his left and right, so everyone on his team knows the new play. This ensures that everyone is where they are supposed to be, and everyone knows what they're supposed to do. This decision has to be made quickly- within seconds (teams receive a penalty if they take too long between downs).

The quarterback can make these split-second decisions because he knows the big-picture strategy, his team's system, and the strengths and weaknesses of the individual players around him. He also knows his playbook by heart (all players memorize their playbooks). Therefore, he knows which tools he has to work with in his tool belt, which levers he can pull. Veteran quarterbacks who have been in the system long enough and have seen enough game situations, can automatically pick up on different patterns and instinctively know what to do in each situation.

The teams with the best playbook (strategy), play-calling (what to do when), and players (execute the play well) will win.

Write Your Own Playbook

You get to write your playbook for your brand of leadership. It can be tailored to your strengths. In life, you're part coach and part quarterback. You see the big picture, you decide the strategy and direction to go towards, and then you execute that plan. As you move through your life and career, you'll navigate a myriad of situations and decision points. As you do, you'll need to "read" the situation and call a play.

This chapter contains twenty short potential "play calls" you can use. They are a combination of frameworks, strategies, tools, mindsets, tips, and tricks. These are the ones that have come up the most or have been the most helpful to leadership teams in business and executive coaching clients. It is certainly not an exhaustive list. I encourage you to create some of your own. As always, take what is useful and discard what is not. Swizzle to make them uniquely your own.

Play: Three Circles

The three circles method helps produce the most favorable outcome in any given situation.

There are, you guessed it, three circles. Picture three circles in a horizontal line. Circle 1 on the left, Circle 2 in the middle,

Circle 3 on the right. They are a math equation. Circle 1 plus Circle 2 equals Circle 3.

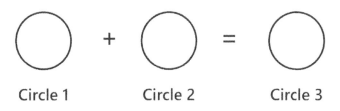

Three Circles Equation

The first circle represents the event or external piece of information. The second circle is your response to the first circle. The third is the outcome.

We often think - and feel - like there is an automatic chain reaction that happens across these three circles. It starts with the first circle and predictably flows through to the third. A person was condescending and rude, I got angry and there was an argument.

This sequence can happen so quickly; it's almost like a reflex. Dr. Russ Harris describes it as being "fused," like a welder fusing metal together.

In reality, Circle 1 is its own little island. It's not connected to Circle 2. There is nothing that *must* happen in Circle 2 depending on what drops in Circle 1. All sorts of things can land in Circle 1 - and it's life - so all kinds of things *will* land in Circle 1.

Circle 2, is where you come in. You own Circle 2. It may mean deciding to do something you don't *feel* like doing, but you are 100% responsible for Circle 2. You're the sheriff of Circle 2, and you run that town.

But wait you might wonder, "Am I not supposed to have any emotions? I can't help if I get angry." No, I'm not asking you to not experience any feelings - you're a human after all, not a robot. And part of being human is having free will and deciding how you will act - even if it is contrary to what we are feeling. Still don't believe me?

Imagine a building on fire. If I say, "Run into that fire," what would you do? You'd probably say no and also hurl a few other choice words in my direction. Why? Because running into a fire is dangerous and scary, and no person in their right mind would run *into* a fire. Now, what if I told you your child or loved one was in the burning building? Would you go? Probably - and probably without me asking. Did the fear go away? Nope. You would feel scared, but you'd *run in any way*. As humans, we can feel one thing and do another.

Let's bring it back to a more practical business setting- say you're in a team meeting. One of your colleagues is rude and condescending. He/she then has an angry outburst in front of everyone. You quickly determine that the best outcome is to keep everyone as calm as possible and get the meeting back on track. So, you decide to calmly and briefly acknowledge the comments your colleague made, maybe addressing some of the legitimate kernels of truth in the statement, and then redirect the conversation to the next steps in the project plan.

You could have decided to respond in a different manner. You could have raised your voice, been rude back to let them know two can play at this game and engaged in a heated argument with that colleague in front of everyone. It might have felt good too, but you choose the action that would bring forth the most favorable outcome.

Using the three circles method does a couple of important things. First, it creates some healthy distance between you and a potentially emotionally charged situation. Second, it requires you to define what you want in the end. And finally, it empowers you because you have control over Circle 2.

A common retort is, "So basically, I just have to fake it?" Yes, to a certain extent. However, it's more an extension of yourself. You're being asked to be the best leader you can be in that moment, which may require you to do things differently than what you had been doing before. Of course, there *will* be times when the universe has conspired against you, and you're just having a crappy day - and, yes, you still need to put on a happy face and do what you need to do. But overall, this approach isn't "faking it," as much as it is stepping into the best version of you.

Pro Tip: Write a "Lincoln Letter" or... email.

Story: *Abraham Lincoln was the president of the United States during the American Civil War. The nation was hanging by a thread, with people fighting and dying across the country. Strong personalities and tempers were flaring among the military and political leaders. This also included members of the cabinet - which was made up of Lincoln's political opponents who thought they should have the top job.*

Lincoln stood in the middle of all this chaos. When he became frustrated and angry, he would pen a "hot" letter and say all the nasty things he wanted to say to someone. Then, he would put it in a drawer and call it a day, letting himself sleep on it. In the morning, he would reread it. If he still wanted to send it, he would. But more often, he would either rewrite the letter or simply not send it at all. When historians opened his papers at the beginning of the 20th century, they discovered a pile of letters with the note, "never sent and never signed."

Lincoln knew writing the first letter served a purpose- to help him diffuse some of his emotions at the moment. Yet, he also understood that he was the leader and head of the nation. This means if he said something regretful, he couldn't take it back. He showed tremendous leadership skills by writing and not sending those letters.

This demonstrates that he knew himself well and he also understood what the ultimate objective is.

Some occasions will call for you to make the unpopular decision at the moment in order to gain the best outcome.

Here's an example:

Let's say you are the Chief Technology Officer at a SaaS company. Your team uses an agile methodology with 2-week sprint cycles. Meaning every two weeks, a group of technology updates pushes live - code updates, bug fixes, new functionality or features, UI/UX enhancements, etc. The technology team pushed a batch of updates live an hour ago. You start getting notified that several clients are saying their online portal is down. You alert your team to begin reviewing the last set of updates and to test multiple account portals to try and identify the scope of the issue.

You're about to dig into reviewing some pieces of the update, when a last-minute emergency call with the leadership team is scheduled. The leaders of the client-facing groups are angry, and they are in a panic. The support teams' phones are ringing off the hook, the Account Managers are trying to save accounts from leaving. Then, the sales team pipes ups and explains they were on a demo with a high-ticket prospect, and the portal went down.

You convey to your colleagues you understand the gravity of the situation and that it is a top-priority for you and your teams. The leader of the support department demands that you write an email response that his team can use to defuse the flood of complaints in their inboxes. He says you caused this issue, but his team is answering for it; so, you need to write down word for word what he and his teams should say.

- What is the most favorable outcome?
  - The client portals need to come back online.
- What can I do right now to get the best outcome? What do I need to say? What do I need to do? How do I need to show up?
  - I need to professionally but firmly let the leader of the support teams know that the best thing for me to do is to start looking into the issue with my teams ASAP.

From there, you might come up with a game plan that looks like this: Let your colleague know you understand what his team is going through by repeating what he has said - the support teams are getting flooded with emails about this issue. State that the best thing for everyone in this situation is for you to get back to your teams ASAP. Doing this will get the client portals back online sooner. To be helpful, you suggest some high-level talking points such as "the technology team is aware of this issue and is actively working to restore access to your online portal as we speak." You also include a few questions he can have his team ask clients that are affected in order to help troubleshoot and how/where to provide that information to you. You let him - and the rest of the leadership team know - when and how you will communicate status updates. Then, you leave the call.

The situation presented and actions taken resulted in short-term frustration from the support department leader, but it was the best call to solve the critical issue. Circle 3 involves keeping the big picture and primary objective in mind.

On other occasions, getting emotional might be the action you *choose* to take in Circle 2.

One time, I had to coordinate team meetings with a global team. I had team members in four different countries and co-ordinating all the time zones and conference rooms was a nightmare. Yet, I thought the monthly meeting with everyone was a good way to make them feel like a team. One group in a certain office location kept arriving late to the meeting. Even more annoying was their nonchalant attitude about being late. When they joined, they didn't apologize or say that they had trouble connecting to the meeting. I believe people should show up on time, especially for scheduled team meetings.

I mentioned it to the group's manager, who was my direct re-port. I could tell she was upset by the situation too. She and I were on the same page about attendance for team meetings. She said she had told them several times that they needed to be on time. She even advised them to block off time before the meeting starts, so they could do test runs with the web conferencing tool we used.

Next team meeting, we both kept an eye out to see if they would arrive on time. They did not. They joined late and even worse, were casually talking and laughing as they joined, interrupting the meeting's flow that had already started.

Afterward, the manager of the group came over to me, embarrassed and exasperated. She repeated that she had told them in no uncertain terms to be on time. I asked what would help at this point, is there anything I could? I'd be happy to back her up on this. She thought about it for a second and, with a little bit of a smile, said, "Well, if *you* told them and were a little...scary...about it, that would probably get them to straighten up and fly right." I laughed and said I could absolutely do that. I'm happy to play the bad cop on certain occasions if it puts my directs in a better position to manage their team.

She then set a meeting with them the next day.

I came into the virtual meeting with a stern face. I said I was there to talk about something that upset me, which needs to be corrected immediately. I described how being late to team meetings was disrespectful to me, to their boss, and to their team members who showed up on time. I told them that being late and disrupting the meeting with their laughing was unacceptable and wasn't going to happen again. I intentionally raised my voice a bit - not yelling, but pronounced - and emphasized the main points by hitting the side of my hand on the table. I said I expect better from this group, and they need to be on time for the next team meeting. Period. I then asked, "Is this clear?" The deafening silence and short and quick nods indicated that they understood. I said "good," and stood up and left. When I was out of the webcam view, I looked back at my manager, trying to stifle a smile.

> Circle 1: Group of team members not showing up to a team meeting on time.

> Desired outcome: For the team members to show up on time.

> Circle 2: Have one of the "big bosses" appear angry to get the point across.

> Circle 3: They were never late again.

To see some more examples of Three Circles, email emily@nextlevel.coach

Play: Level-Up

Continuously grow and develop your skills. Reinvent and reinvest in progress. Whether it's taking a course on a specific, tangible skill or doing the internal work on your mental game and emotional intelligence, have the mindset of always learning and improving. Curiosity in other fields may make you more innovative in your own. Anything that makes you a better person as a whole will naturally carry over and make you a better leader.

> **Quote**: *"The ability to learn is the most important quality a leader can have."*
> - *Padmasree Warrior, CEO & Founder at Fable*

Play: Double-Down on Strengths

A good leader is self-aware enough to know his strengths and weaknesses. Move into areas and set up situations where you can use skills that come naturally to you and where you contribute the most.

Don't be threatened by people who you feel do something better than you. Instead, seek those people out and actively recruit them.

Think of a basketball team, let's say you're a 5'8" point guard - you're quick, you're fast, you have crazy good ball-handling skills. But you are not good at rebounds - you'd get killed in the paint if you tried to out jump an opposing forward or center. Now you can try to get better in this area. But even if you have the perfect technique for boxing out, you probably won't outdo someone who is more naturally suited to that position.

If you only played with players who are just like you, then your team would get crushed. Your team would consist of one type of player – a whole bunch of 5'8" point guards. Instead, you need to find a big, strong 6'7" forward who can dominate the boards.

Different skill sets along with different strengths work together to produce a winning team.

A good leader knows his strengths and weaknesses. *A great leader knows how to use them.*

Story: *I'm not a visionary. I can't typically see something that is not there - a new invention, creating a new entity in the ecosystem, etc - but I love people who can - they have brought us AirPods, K-Cups, and Uber. However, my real strength is setting the strategy and bringing together all the components of the tactical execution to make these visions a reality.*

I've been lucky enough to work with some exceptional companies whose founders had great vision for a business idea or new niche in the market. One co-founder, in particular, we'll call him Jamal, oozed charisma. He had a presence when he walked into a room, and he loved talking to people. The topic he liked to talk about the most was himself and he didn't have any issues with confidence or the notions of self-importance. His charisma could easily turn into arrogance and bravado and definitely ruffled some feathers. Still, when he gave his attention to someone, he had the ability to make that person feel like the most important person in the world.

He had used these traits to sell the vision of his company in the beginning stages. He and his other co-founders saw an opportunity for a new type of entity in the industry. In the early years, it required "selling the dream" to reluctant audiences even though a lot of the business infrastructure had not been built yet. It was because of this vision and ability to persuade, that the company had grown and done very well.

Years later, through a series of circumstances, a new leadership team had come in to replace the original founders. I was rising through the ranks and was one of the promising young guns and a fledgling leader at that point. The company was now transitioning into a larger, more mature business. Jamal was transitioning out of the business - partly on his own volition, partly not.

I'll always remember a rare quiet moment when he came into my office and we were talking about the direction of the business. I knew what was happening with his exit and was trying to be gracious and generous by saying, "You know this company owes a lot to you. None of us would be here if you'd hadn't started it." He paused for a moment, looked down, looked back up, and said, "Right now, what you bring to the table is more important to this company." I was shocked. I'd never seen this side of him. He knew that his strengths - his big personality, charisma, and ability to sell the dream in order to get their first customers - got the company off the ground. Yet, he also knew that there are more capable people who could take the company to the next level.

Play: Have a Plan So You Can Change the Plan

> **Quote:** *"Everybody has a plan until they get punched in the mouth."*
>
> *- Mike Tyson*

Have a plan. Take a reasonable amount of time to think about where you want to go and how you're going to get there. Then, know that your plan will change.

If you're a "fly by the seat of your pants, variety is the spice of life" type of person, remind yourself to take time to put an initial plan together. It doesn't need to be detailed. It can be a high-level overview. Just make sure you're at least headed in the right general direction, and you've thought through some of the big pieces or considerations.

If you're an "uber-organized, let me color-code everything" type of person, remind yourself that not knowing exactly when and how every single step will happen is okay. Come up with your initial plan and realize, at some point, you just have to start and adapt as you go.

Imagine standing in the doorway of a vast dimly lit room. You can only see very far in front of you. You're going to walk across the floor to the other side of the room. It would make sense to at least figure out what wall you're trying to reach, right? So you will at least know the general direction you will be going. Now, imagine that this room has a hexagonal grid pattern on the floor. The hexagon you're standing on lights up, and you can only see the borders of the surrounding tiles. You decide on your next step. Then, that set of surrounding tiles appear. You determine your next step, and the process continues.

> **Pro Tip:** When you start taking steps in a certain direction, let go of any specific expectation of the result. Meaning, if an action or series of steps doesn't get you to exactly where you thought it would, that's fine. Keep your eyes open to the best next steps. What's the best decision you can make now with all the information you have at the time?

Play: Change Your Mind

You have the right to change your mind. It is okay - and sometimes very smart - to change your mind. A lot of people have strong notions of not quitting, finishing what they start, not giving up, and not being irresponsible. These are good and even noble attitudes but can be detrimental if applied to the wrong scenario.

Don't waste time in a bad situation when you can change it.

Story: *I had a client take a voluntary board seat. He was very excited at the prospect. He did it with the best intentions, and accepting the offer was the best decision he could have made at the time. Then, after a month or two, he found it was a toxic environment, and the work itself was not what he had originally anticipated.*

However, the thought of leaving created mountains of guilt and resentment. "I just can't quit, that's not what I do, that's not who I am," he would think. He would also entertain thoughts like, "If they just changed and did what they're supposed to do, everything would be fine." After several months of this, it finally reached a tipping point, and he decided to resign.

It felt like a dam breaking. He felt so relieved, describing how he physically felt lighter and had more energy. Looking back, he said the environment was an infuriating, demoralizing drain of energy and he couldn't figure out why he stayed so long.

Having the foresight and fortitude to change your mind can be what's best for you and the people around you.

Don't be flippant with this. Don't use it as an excuse to just give up on something without trying or running away whenever something gets hard. Use the spirit of making the best decision you can at the time. Then, when new information presents itself, ask the question again and reassess as needed. If it is still the best decision, great. If it's not the best decision anymore, make a new one.

Play: Do It for You

Do things because you want to do them, not because you think that is what you're "supposed" to do or what other people expect of you. I'm not talking about paying taxes or comforting an abandoned baby. Do *those* things. But if you're making career decisions or choosing where and how to spend your time, ask yourself:

- Why am I doing this?
- Who am I doing this for?
- Am I truly doing this for *me*?

If the answer contains the word "should," it may be something to take a look at. Should can be an external expectation being placed on you. A common answer is, "Well, I'm doing this because that's just what you should do…" It also has endless variations: "It's just what you're supposed to do when you get to this point…" or, "I know that's what everyone is supposed to do…"

> **Quote:** *"Don't wake up in the morning, walk out the door, and should all over yourself."*
>
> *- A common saying used in coaching.*

Another big hint here is if you find yourself saying or implying, "everyone should" do something, or everyone should think a certain way. This line can come in the form of, "Everyone knows you're supposed to do X." Or maybe, "Anyone would do Y, in that situation," or even, "I know everyone would say I'm supposed to do Z."

First of all, those are pretty big assumptions you're making for the rest of the human race.

Secondly, and more importantly, it's your life. No one else has to live it. No one else *gets* to live it. And this ain't no dress rehearsal.

Play: Spend Your Time Wisely

Your focus and attention should be at the intersection of: "Things That Matter" and "Things You Can Control." This means anything that falls in the middle, or overlaps, are things to take note of. Everything else can be put on the backburner or discarded.

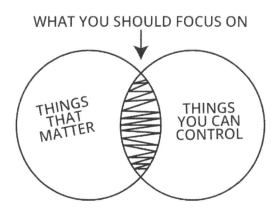

Quick reminder for where to spend your time.

- Does this matter?
- Is this (really) a big deal?
- Is this in my sphere of influence?
- Can I do something about it right now?

If you answer no to any of these questions, drop it like it's hot. Those worries are literally not worth one second of your time or ounce of your energy. If you answer yes to those questions, then great. Now, you have to decide what your next step is and what action you'll need to take.

You have a finite amount of mental energy each day. You need to spend it where it's most useful. Don't spin your wheels on distractions.

Play: Make It a Hell Yes or Hard No

A challenge for a lot of driven and successful people is they want to do everything. They want to sign up for that class, get that degree, read that book, read *all* the books, start a business, help someone with their business, and the list goes on. When asked for something, they'll default to "Yes." While a "yes" can be good in the right places, default yeses can hurt you.

When one of my clients realized she had been automatically saying yes all her life, she then thought back through all the paths she had gone down. She then said, "Man, my automatic yeses have been killing me." She had been very successful despite this (not because of it). However, she decided to make her default "no" to allow her more focus, time, and energy towards what she really wanted to pursue. She in turn had more free time to dedicate towards her highest priority goals.

> **Pro Tip:** *Helping others is a good thing but remember saying "no" once in a while will give you more freedom.*

Time is something you can't get back and can't make more of. Set your threshold for how you use it extremely high.

A quick, easy question to ask is, "Does this bring me closer to my goal(s) or further away?" If it brings you closer, say yes, and do it. If it takes you further away, say no.

If you prefer something more involved, I'd recommend using this rubric from *Essentialism*:

OPPORTUNITY
What opportunity is being offered to you?

MINIMUM
What are your minimum criteria for this option to be considered?

EXTREME
What are the ideal criteria for this option to be approved?

One way to assess opportunities.

You will need *all* the minimum boxes and *two* of the extreme boxes to move forward.

Play: Break It Down...Way Down

High achievers often have big, audacious goals - which is excellent. Thinking big enough to have a dream that seems out of reach is one hallmark of a visionary leader.

Making that vision a reality will often require you to break up the plan into smaller steps. Compare these tasks:

"Go create a multi-million dollar business!"

"Go research how to register your business entity with the state."

"Go lose 30 pounds!"

"Go put your walking shoes by the door for tomorrow morning."

Take the big goal and reverse-engineer or back into your next step. First, break it up into the broadest chunks. Then take the first big chunk and break that down further into medium categories. Then, take the medium category and break it down into what needs to happen this month, this week, today and right now. If a step seems too big, break it down into smaller steps.

What is the smallest baby step you can take right now? What makes you go, "Oh, that's it? That's easy! I can do that." That's the one you'd want to start with; do that. And then, continue to do that over and over again.

Pro Tip: *Create mini-habits. These are tiny things you do regularly. The goal is to keep the habit. A mini-habit can be something like reading two pages of a book a day. Even on your busiest days, you know you can read two pages. Some days you might read more which is great. However, even on the days you only do the minimum, you kept up the habit. Mission accomplished.*

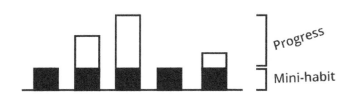

Mini-habits add up.

Quote: *"Small wins add up faster than you think."*

- Emily Sander

Play: Love the Process

A trick to success is finding ways to love *the process*. Pick your end goals wisely at the beginning. Make sure you have your ladder up against the right wall, then focus on, and take joy in, the day-to-day process that's getting you there.

Many people only think about the end goal. They visualize accomplishing that goal and how it will look and feel. They rely on that for motivation to get them through the journey, which is good and certainly part of the equation. It will work some of the time, but not all the time. If it is a long-term goal (say a few years), then it can seem too far away. It's easy to put something off today because you don't feel like doing it or you don't think it will make that much of a difference. If you focus on making each step fun and enjoyable, then you will look forward to the day-to-day process instead of dreading it completely.

What would make the process fun?

What would make you look forward to, and want to do the activity everyday?

> **Story:** *Take this book as an example. Writing and editing this book is not a one and done deal. It has taken numerous writing sessions. I had to create extra time in my day. The best time from a scheduling perspective is in the morning. I got up an hour earlier each weekday to write before work. I'm not a morning person by nature, so for me to get up early, sometimes I thought about the*

end result. I thought about having a published book and how good that accomplishment would feel.

However, most of the time, finding ways to look forward to what's right in front of me is more helpful. For instance, I take a short walk before I write. I've gotten to the point where I like my early morning walk - it feels good. It wakes up my brain, gets my blood flowing, and I get to breathe in some fresh air. I look forward to my short walk. When I get back, I go to my newly designated writing area. I like slipping on my Bose noise-canceling headphones and playing some designated music tracks. When I listen to these beats, it puts me in the mood to write. When I'm done writing, I will take another walk. It doesn't matter whether I liked what I wrote or not, all that mattered was that I kept up the habit and wrote that day. During my victory lap, I feel great going into the rest of the day because I've already made progress towards my goal while most people are still fast asleep.

Collectively, I love my new routine. Of course, the byproduct is writing more and more of my book.

Play: Get Outside Your Comfort Zone (but Not Too Much)

Most have heard the mantra "get outside your comfort zone." This is true. I'd add a secondary note to that, which is "but not too far." You need to step outside your comfort zone to improve, but getting *too* far outside of it may defeat the purpose. You want to stay in your sweet spot of growth.

Imagine you are training for a marathon, but you have never run before. Attempting to run the entire 26 miles in your first go would undoubtedly be outside your comfort zone. But, you'd probably get incredibly sore and injure yourself. If you expected to run the entire 26 miles and fell short, it could be discouraging.

Instead, you may want to walk or run just one mile for your first training session. One mile is also outside of your comfort zone, but it's not too far out. It's optimal for growth.

Here's another analogy: If you stretch a rubber band a medium amount, it will expand and do its job correctly. If you pull it too far, it will break and become useless. You want to stretch yourself, but not so far that you'll snap and break.

Another good way to measure if you are doing it right is by the way you feel. Look for that perfect cocktail of fear and excitement - that jolt of energy where you're scared, but you also know that this push is good for you. Say yes to these opportunities before you can talk yourself out of them.

> **Quote:** *"I didn't think I would be prime minister...But there will be a moment when someone asks you to do something beyond your comfort zone. I am not unique."*
>
> *- Jacinda Ardern, Prime Minister of New Zealand*

Play: Play With People Out of Your League

> **Quote:** *"If you're the smartest person in the room, you're in the wrong room."*
>
> *- Lorne Michaels*

Play with people who are better than you. This may require leaving your ego at the door, but it's a vital part of growing into the best leader you can. Find someone or a group of people who have a skill or trait that you want. Hang out with them, spend time with them, watch what they do. If you don't know this person personally, read about them, listen to any interviews with them, etc.

Here is an interesting axiom most people should hear: "You become the aggregate of the five people you spend the most time around." So take a look around and make sure that those closest to you are pulling you up, not down. Find someone who has achieved what you want to achieve and ask him/her how he/she did it. This person's path might not be the exact path you take, but you will likely learn some useful guideposts on how to move forward.

Don't rest on your laurels or become complacent. Keep giving yourself an edge.

Story: My dad played tennis when he was younger. He was 6'5", strong and apparently had a wicked serve and volley. He won several state tournaments. He once told me about the times he practiced with Tom Gorman. Tom was a professional tennis player who ranked 8th in the world and reached the semi-finals at Wimbledon, the US Open, and the French Open in the early 70s. Tom would show up at the local courts my dad played at and would ask kids to practice with him. Dad would volunteer.

My dad shakes his head and smiles when he recounts practicing with Tom. Tom would ask the kids to help him with his conditioning - he'd tell them to make him run around a lot to try and wear him out. Dad would give it all he had, full effort, hitting the ball as hard as he could, putting on all his best moves. Yet, it was no contest for Tom. He would win every time. And to top it all off, he did so wearing ankle weights! But Dad upped his game by playing with one of the best around.

Play: Get a Pep Talk

Sometimes a good old fashioned pep talk *does* work. I would not have this as your only means of motivation, but it's a good one to have in your back pocket in case you need it. Listen to a song that gets you pumped up. Read a speech or a quote that inspires you. Look at a specific picture that motivates you and gives you extra energy.

Story: After graduating from university, I got a congressional internship in Washington, DC for the summer. Towards the end of my internship, I had applied for another job back home in Seattle. I had gotten an interview. As I was preparing for it, I was feeling quite nervous. All my answers were very professional, polished, by the book, and humble (I really didn't like to brag).

My internship coordinator was nice enough to help me prep for the interview. After I read her some of my notes, she squinted her eyes and pursed her lips and said, "Um, let's go to lunch."

As we ate our sandwiches at a nearby deli, she told me, "You need to come at this interview way different."

"Okay…" I said, not quite understanding.

"In fact," she said in between bites, "you need to think of yourself way different."

"Um, okay, what do you mean…?"

"How would you feel if you were talking to someone giving these answers?" I thought to myself, pretty good. My answers sound prepared and they showcase the skills I have without being arrogant.

She put down her sandwich, brought her hands together in a steeple in front of her face, and said, "You are the shit. Do you understand?"

No. No, I did not. I'm young, inexperienced, and I've done nothing so far; I need a job and will take one from anyone who will hire me.

She went on to say, "You graduated from a good college, you just completed a very selective internship - do you know how many people applied to this? Do you know how many people I interviewed? We picked you, and you rocked it. You are the shit. They would be lucky to have you."

I remember that moment very vividly. Until then, the thought had never occurred to me. I had always had it the other way around in my head - I hope they will like me. I hope I will get in. I hope I'm good enough. She had flipped that thought on its head. I was special. I was a top candidate, and they are lucky that I'm interested in the role.

As she saw it start to sink in, she told me to say it. "Say what?" I asked.

"Say you're the shit."

"I'm the shit," I said flatly and quietly, almost as a question.

"No, c'mon say it like you mean it."

"I'm the shit."

She motioned with both her hands to up the intensity.

"I'm the shit!"

"You're the f**king shit."

"I'm the shit," I repeated in what was becoming a Jerry MacGuire "Show me the money" type moment. I even got a few sideways glances from the nearest tables.

"You're about to interview for this job; what are you?"

"The shit!"

"Good."

Play: Put in the Reps

There comes a point in the planning process where you just have to put in the work. You've done all the research, you've done all the planning, everything is set up just so. Now, you have to do the work.

As Malcolm Gladwell posited, it takes 10,000 hours to gain mastery of something. Put in the practice. Put in the time.

An example of this came up while I was learning about different aspects of financial investing. One way to research and evaluate companies and their stock is through technical analysis. This method involves reviewing the stock chart - if you look up a company's ticker symbol and see the graph with a line going up and down showing the stock's price movement, that is the chart. There are visual patterns the line makes that some say can predict the probability of the next price move. These technical analysts will look at the chart pattern and place their buy or sell orders off of what they see.

There is a seemingly endless list of factors you can learn about - different indicators (besides price) you can plot on the chart, various formats of the chart, which timeframe to look at, etc. You need to learn about these to a certain extent in order to not be reckless. Finding the indicators, type of chart, and timeframe that suit your investing style is a crucial step.

After that, there comes a point when you just need to start looking at charts every day. Reviewing the charts gives you the repetition you need to start seeing patterns and trends. Investors who are just beginning might need to look at a chart for several minutes, actually drawing lines on the chart to see what the pattern is. Expert investors can flip through a series of charts, only glancing at each one for a second or two, and see the pattern in their heads in no time. They've seen so many, and they can interept all the data coming off the chart in near real-time. They've put in the reps.

> **Quote**: *"Sometimes magic is just someone spending more time on something than anyone else might reasonably expect."*
> *- Raymond Joseph Teller, of Penn & Teller on the process of master*

Play: Act Confidently

> **Quote**: *"Rule 1: The actions of confidence come first; the feelings of confidence come later."*
> *- Russ Harris, The Happiness Trap*

Don't wait until you *feel* confident to do something or else you may be waiting forever. You have to *act* confidently first, then the feeling will come next. To learn more about this, I'd highly recommend Russ Harris's books (*The Happiness Trap* and *The Confidence Gap*.) The central premise is *doing* things will make you confident. Do the thing you want to do as confidently as you can. Each time you do it, you will gain more confidence compared to the last time.

Take tying your shoes, for instance. Most people reading this book probably didn't have to drum up a high level of courage to tie their shoes today. You just did it. However, when you were first learning, it was a daunting task that was done under the supervision of an adult. The outcome wasn't certain. You might tie your shoes correctly; you might not. Each time you did it, your confidence grew and now you're 100% confident you'll tie them correctly each time.

Story: *I remember a time at a previous job, when I was taking on a new role. As part of my new role, I was given many new tasks. One of them was to deliver a training call on how to use our online platform. This role was passed on to me by a veteran in the company. She was kind enough to let me sit in and listen to several of her trainings. I took copious notes. Then, the first training that I was going to be in charge of got scheduled for a week out. I must have practiced a dozen times. On the day of the training, I was nervous - it was a new client; I* *wanted to make sure he knew how to use the platform. Not only that, but I wanted this new client to have a positive first experience with the company. When the time came, I practically read the "script" I had made for myself. The training went fine, but I was emotionally spent afterward.*

Years later, I ended up running the department and had my team members give the training sessions. I needed to train the team members on how to deliver the training I had been giving. I coordinated calendars with one of my new hires, inviting him to a client training so he could listen in. For one particular training, I was in back-to-back meetings right before it. I had to jump right on the call with zero prep time, which was completely fine. I got on the call with zero anxiety, worry, or nervousness. The call went smoothly, and the client was excited to be on the platform. By that time, I'd probably given a hundred training sessions. I could do it on the fly with no notes.

After that meeting ended, my new hire asked me all sorts of questions. Some of the questions were the same ones I had asked years before. A big smile broke out across my face as I realized and remembered that feeling. I like to tell this story because it's a reminder that no matter how big, arduous and nerve-wracking something may seem, it won't always feel that way. What scares you today, you will be able to do with your eyes closed one day. Then, you'll look back and smile at yourself.

> **Pro Tip:** *Remember, you don't have to "hustle for your self-worth." No one will ever be better at being you than you. You can always be 100% confident in that.*

Play: Remember You Can Figure It Out and Handle It

This play is arguably the most important one. What-if scenarios can throw us all for a loop. What if this happens? What if that happens? What if I don't get that job? What if I do get that job? What if I bomb this meeting? What if we don't hit numbers? What if so-and-so quits? This deluge of questioning goes on and on. You could run hypothetical scenarios forever with different combinations.

Take a second and think back to a time when you had a big what-if situation or decision staring you in the face. Most people have too many of these to count. And they all ended with some version of "and then I handled it" or "and then I figured it out." If they didn't, you wouldn't be here.

Imagine an aerial shot of the river delta streams fanning out before you. Infinite possibilities as the main river breaks off into little side streams of potential realities. Instead of thinking of all the possible side streams that can form, rest knowing that they all end in the ocean of "and then I handled it, and then I figured it out."

When you get tempted to start running on the what-if hamster wheel, use the river analogy to remind yourself that you will figure it out. Point your energy towards that belief, and rest a little easier.

> **Pro Tip**: *Instead of asking "What If," ask "What Is."*
>
> *What is happening right now?*
> *Where are you right now?*
> *What do I know to be true right now?*
> *Is there anything I need to do right now?*
>
> *Bring yourself back into the present.*

Play: Be. Do. Have.

Many people think about a goal from the perspective of "I want to have X." I want to have a dream job. I want to have a big paycheck. I want that house. I want to make better decisions. I want to be more confident.

Some people stop there and demand it from the world. They might look around and ask, "Who will give this to me?" Some people go a step further and try to figure out what they need *to do* to get what they want. While this is better than just stopping at the first question, rarely do people make it to the third-level question: Who do I need to *be*?

Instead of looking to external factors outside of yourself, think inward.

What kind of person does those things?
What kind of person has those things?
What type of person attracts the things I want?
What qualities would draw those things in?
Who do I need to become?

Play: Assign the Meaning

You get to assign the meaning. This play is especially helpful right after something "bad" happens. For example, let's say you got laid off. Most people would consider this a bad thing. Here are two ways you can go about this:

1. This is the worst thing that could have happened. This is the end.
2. This is the catalyst for me to find a new (and possibly better) job. This is the beginning of my next chapter.

Which one sounds better to you?

You might not be able to control what happens to you, but you do have a big label gun in your hand. This means you get to assign the meaning to everything that happens to you. No matter what happens, no one can take away your label gun.

Play: Pay It Forward

A person can have all the talent in the world. They can put in all the hard work, but they still might need a door to be opened for them. Many people just need that first break - that one person to take a chance on them and give them a shot - and they will be off to the races.

As a leader, it's your job and privilege to look for these opportunities. Look for people in your organization who may be untapped talent. When the time is right, open a door for them.

I was very fortunate to have someone do this for me early in my career. I remember sitting in my boss and mentor's office and thanking him profusely for the opportunity and asking sincerely if there's anything I can ever do to repay him. Without missing a beat, he said, "There is something." I look at him intently, paying close attention. He continued, "When you get the chance to do this for someone else, pay it forward. I was in your seat once and asked the person who gave me my first break the same thing. He said, pay it forward. So now, I'm saying it to you."

Ever since then, I've looked for people to pay it forward to. And I must say, as grateful and exhilarating as it was to get my good break - opening a door for someone else and seeing them succeed is an equally, if not more amazing experience. It's a great way to make a meaningful, positive, and lasting contribution.

Pro Tip: *Make it clear to your leadership team that you expect them to actively look for these high-potential folks as well. Good leadership teams know who their rising stars are.*

Play: Have Fun

Quote: *"If you don't have fun, what's the point?"*
- Anonymous

This play is an essential one. Many business leaders get sucked into tunnel vision very quickly - whatever is happening with the business at that moment is *all* that's happening; whatever the monthly numbers are, whatever the client escalation is that's *the* most important thing. Sometimes, it's hard to see beyond that.

And, yes, it's important to try to do your best work. In fact, some of the work you do may be serious work. But as the saying goes, "Take the work seriously, don't take yourself seriously."

Imagine having a leader who never smiles or jokes or laughs. Imagine someone who is always stern and down on whatever is happening now. Most people aren't going to want to work for that person. Instead, try to see the light side and humor in things. Have fun in the right moments.

As a leader, you may have to *generate the fun*. As Brendon Burchard says, "The power plant doesn't *have* energy; it *generates* energy." You may have to create the fun. Don't wait for it to land on you or your team.

Story: *In a work setting, I'm naturally serious. Some people describe me as "all business" or "very business-y." When I landed my first role where I had to manage people, which was a great joy but also stressful, I was talking to one of my peers and about how the week was going. She said, "It seems like it's been a pretty brutal week for you." I told her it had actually been a great week. I'd had some very good one-on-one meetings with people, everyone was collaborative, the group found some creative ways to get projects done, and I was pleased about how everything was going. She then said, "Well, you need to inform your face."*

Her response is funny because I'm also naturally expressive. Numerous people in my life have told me I should never play poker - my face will give me away. But I realized, sometimes at work, I can have a very stoic look. It can be placid and hard to read. I don't mean for this to happen; it's not because I'm uncaring or trying to do it, it's just my face. In certain situations, it can even be a good thing - confused panic can come across as calm resolve. But there are times I do need to inform my face – and generate positive energy for my team.

When you look back, you won't remember the client escalations or the Q2 numbers that one year. Most people remember the experiences they had with people - a funny moment at lunch with colleagues, a feeling of solidarity when a group of you stayed up late to work on a project together, weird nicknames that become an inside joke, etc.

Don't take these for granted. Recognize and cherish these moments when they happen. Participate in them, and when possible, generate them.

I once heard an actor who was asked why he did what he did. He said he did it because once in a while, there is the perfect combination of the right director, cast, and crew and that brief period of time on set when it's just "more fun than fun."

Key Takeaways:
- You get to make your own playbook.
- You are part coach and part player.
- Be intentional and selective in creating your playbook and calling plays.

Key Questions:
- What playbook or system is best suited to your strengths and style?
- Which play calls would you benefit the most from adding to your playbook?
- Which play calls would you like to stop running?

PART TWO

BUSINESS LESSONS AND APPLICATIONS

Part two provides real-world business practices for you and for your team. It covers some lessons on communication and how to deliver information effectively. It ends with tactical, hands-on suggestions and examples for recruiting and asking powerful questions.

CHAPTER 5

YOU AS A LEADER

"If you can't tell me what you're doing and why in less than 60 seconds, it's because you're not thinking clearly."

- Ruth Porat, CFO at Alphabet and Google

Decide

As a leader, you get paid to make decisions that other people can't or won't. As you move up, you'll need to make more decisions with incomplete or imperfect data, and the decisions that come across your desk will get more complicated. Sometimes, the decisions won't be clear-cut. As in, you will have to pick the *least bad* option, or you will have to pick what you know will be an unpopular decision. At the highest levels, individual choices can make or break the business.

Executive leadership requires *action*.

Become an expert at making decisions. It's a skill like any other - practice, put in the reps, apply the lessons from last time - and you will become more comfortable and confident.

While it's almost always better to do - or at least try - something, knowing your tendencies will help when making decisions. If you're cautious and risk-averse by nature, then you may need to make decisions more quickly than you're comfortable with. If you tend to make knee-jerk reactions and are a risk-seeker, then it may benefit you to take some extra time to think through.

> **Quote:** "If a decision is reversible, the biggest risk is moving too slow. If a decision is irreversible, the biggest risk is moving too fast."
>
> - *James Clear*

Think of the well-known phrase "Ready, Aim, Fire." Some people sit there and go, "Ready, get ready, keep getting ready, are we ready?" They are in a perpetual paralysis analysis loop. Others go, "Fire, aim, why weren't you ready?" This sequence can be equally ineffective if you're blindly firing in desperate hopes of hitting something. The best version is a steady, consistent series of: "Ready, Aim, Fire. Ready, Aim, Fire." Decide, Assess, Adapt. Decide, Assess, Adapt.

Make the best decision you can with all the information you have at the time. See what new scenario unfolds. Then, make the next best decision you can with all the information you have at the time. Keep moving forward, don't second-guess yourself or get consumed by doubt.

Remember, people like and respect leaders who know when to act and will make tough decisions. If people like and respect you (respect being the most important), they will follow you.

Don't Let Perfect Be the Enemy of Good

I have a streak of perfectionism in me. I want everything to be high-quality. I want things double and triple checked for accuracy. I want results and work products to be impressively good. That is a good thing. A very good thing actually...to an extent. There's a tipping point where working on something further is a waste of time. You've reached the point of diminishing returns - where the effort you are putting into it is not going to make enough of a difference to be worth it. At this stage, you're unnecessarily delaying a project. You're just creating more work for yourself and your team. Where is the tipping point? It depends. It's on a sliding scale, depending on the project. If you're performing brain surgery, please double and triple check things. If you're working on a PowerPoint presentation and spending time aligning the left margin 1/10th a degree, move on.

Be aware when *done* is better than perfect.

Know Your MVP and Be Agile

A helpful approach to take is MVP (Minimally Viable Product). This concept is often used for building the first version of a product. Get the MVP to market and see if the core functionality is intriguing and attractive enough to buy. It prevents wasting time and capital on building a product no one wants. If it works, it allows you to collect feedback from early adopters. Once you get the feedback, then you can quickly work on the next iterations of the product.

Many product teams work within an agile methodology. This methodology stipulates you should produce the most value to the business as quickly as possible. Once an MVP is established, the product team will work in a series of "sprints" - this can be two-week intervals where a small update or enhancement is completed and delivered. You don't get the finished product with all the bells and whistles, but you will have a working product and you can adjust it quickly if needed.

The MVP concept works outside of the product world as well.

Ask yourself, "What's the MVP?" What is the minimum required to get this project or deliverable off the ground?

"What is good enough?" This may sound like a cop-out, and I'm certainly not encouraging anyone to do shoddy work intentionally. However, good enough by definition is *good enough*.

Sometimes, done is better than perfect. Sometimes, just starting is better than perpetually planning. Don't overcomplicate things.

Protect the Asset!

> **Quote**: *"We think, mistakenly, that success is the result of the amount of time we put in at work, instead of the quality of time we put in."*
>
> *- Ariana Huffington*

Protect the asset. Here's a hint: the asset is *you*. This is another excellent concept from the author of *Essentialism*, Greg McKeown. Self-care is important for everyone, but it is especially important for leaders. The definition of self-care is, "taking action to preserve one's own health." It seems basic, but a lot of us forget or deprioritize it.

You're making the big decisions. You're interacting with numerous teams, and people are looking to you to set the direction and tone which means you need to make sure you are at your best.

When I bring self-care up, I almost always run into a version of this response: "Yeah, yeah, I know, but there's *so* much to do. Now that I'm in this role, I have to work harder and do more; I can't let anyone down." Let's just get this out of the way now. It is not selfish to take care of yourself. Repeating for emphasis - it is *not* selfish to take care of yourself. It's smart. It's prudent. It's *part of your job*. And quite frankly, it's irresponsible not to.

Imagine a person who has slept an average of four hours a night for the last month. He has been holed up in an office for 18 hours a day; it's dark when he comes in and dark when he leaves. He has looked at nothing but a revolving door of computer, iPad, and phone screens. He thinks about nothing but what's going on at work. He is taking on mountains of stress. He hoovers up the most convenient meal or snack while taking back-to-back calls. He chugs coffee and Redbull all day but still manages to have dark circles under his eyes.

Now. Imagine this person has an important decision to make that will significantly affect you, your livelihood, and your family. How do you feel about that?

It would be like a singer going out on tour after smoking, drinking, staying up 20 hours a day for a week. How would this singer perform at her concert? What would her voice be like? Would that be fair to her audience? The singer's voice is her *asset,* which means the singer should protect it.

As a leader, you are the asset. You are the mechanism through which your leadership expresses itself. Taking charge of this process is a sign of strength. You are setting yourself *and the people around you* up for success.

I'm not saying there won't be times when you have to stay late or put in extra hours. I'm not saying there won't be stressful times. And, no, I'm not saying there won't be nights where you just don't get a lot of sleep. These are all reality at certain points. I'm saying be cognizant of this and be mature enough to manage it.

Be self-aware enough to know where you are. If you know you've been short on sleep recently and you're a little more tired and stressed than usual, keep that in mind. On these days, give people a little more slack than you feel like, catch yourself if you're about to let a zinger fly, push a big decision to the next day if possible, or take an extra minute or two to think about it and get some more clarity.

Pro Tip: *Some people don't like the term "self-care." They think it sounds soft. Another way to think about this is "priming" yourself or "turbo-charging" yourself.*

Find something outside of work you like doing. Even if you have the dream job where you are passionate about your work, it's good to have hobbies outside of that. Having different interests is a great way to gain some perspective, and it will give your brain something else to think about for a while. Examples of this are the gym, hiking, learning a new language, computer games, sky-diving, underwater basket weaving, and so much more. The activity doesn't matter. Whatever does it for you, go do these things, and block it off in your calendar if needed.

Pro Tip: Sometimes, protecting the asset does include watching Netflix on the couch. Not every hour of every day, but an occasional "lazy weekend" where you don't "do" anything is exactly what's needed.

Your brain and body need rest to perform at their best. Incorporating periods of active rest promotes better and more sustained performance.

Play the long game; play the smart game. What makes you the best leader? What makes you perform at your best? What sets you up to be successful?

Responsible vs. Accountable

Quote: "As a leader, you are in charge of an outcome. As you move up, if you try to micromanage, you're going to die."

- Ed Barton, CEO

As you move to new leadership levels, the notion of "what got you here won't get you there" comes into play. Meaning, the skills that made you excel at your old role aren't necessarily the ones that will make you excel in your next position. You will be less involved in certain types of work and more involved in others.

As Scott Eblin outlines in his book, *The Next Level*, the further you move up, the more time and energy should be spent on acquiring *leadership* skills vs. *technical* skills.

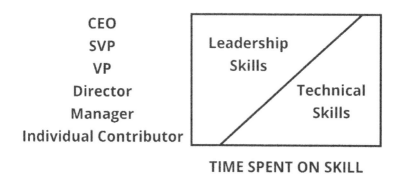

The required skillsets change with new roles.

This adjustment can range from new and exciting, to jarring and frightening. The first (and usually most significant) jump is a high-performing individual contributor who moves to a manager role. This transition occurs when an individual moves from being good at production work to overseeing people and processes. Success no longer derives from how good they can *personally* do something; it now comes from how successful they can guide and facilitate their *team* to a goal.

This adjustment happens at other inflection points as well. Some common examples are when a leader becomes a manager of *other* people's managers or when someone is put in charge of a department outside their functional area of expertise.

All of these involve moving from responsibility to accountability.

Mowing the Lawn

A helpful analogy to keep in mind here is mowing the lawn. Let's say you start by being responsible for mowing five lawns a day. You have the biggest, most complex lawns to mow because you're the best lawnmower. You know your five lawns inside and out. You know the most effective and efficient ways to cut the lawns and all the nuances of getting the edges just right to keep them looking gorgeous. Then, you get promoted, and suddenly, you are in charge of 500 lawns. You can't possibly mow 500 lawns a day yourself. So you need to hire a team of the best lawn mowers and set up the best processes to make sure all the lawns get mowed. You still know how and are able to mow individual lawns yourself, but that is no longer the best use of your time. The best use of your time is hiring and training the best lawn mowers, coordinating schedules, etc.

The responsibility of "I cut the grass" moves to the accountability of "The grass got cut."

Letting others be responsible for something can cause some anxiety. Whether it's performing a technical skill, leading a meeting, managing a project, or managing a person. Keep in mind that not everyone will perform on the same level as you. As in, not everyone will do things the way you would do it. *And that is okay.* If it produces a positive result, it's okay. Remember that there are a hundred different ways to do something; it doesn't have to be yours. If someone makes a mistake (that you never would!), know that it is part of the learning process. Let them fail forward. Teach and guide them to loop up and get better.

As a leader, people skills matter more than technical skills.

Pro Tip: *Ask yourself, "What can I do now that others can't?"*

Given your role, what are you able to do that your team members cannot? Do you have access to certain information they don't? Can you make certain decisions they can't?

These activities usually hint at where you should spend time. If three different people can do or decide Item A and only you can carry out or make a call on Item B, then you should be putting energy into Item B.

Commander's Intent

The "commander's intent" is a military term that says soldiers should always know the overall goal or objective of their leader. In the military, the commander may die in battle, or communication lines can break down. The rest of the unit can't stand around aimlessly while they're getting shot at. Soldiers need to be able to make decisions on their own to complete the mission. To do this, they must know what their leader *intended* to do and then figure out the best way to do that given their circumstances.

As a business leader, everyone on your team should know what you're trying to do. They should know what the overall business objective of the company is and how their business unit aligns with it. They should be provided enough information and context to make informed decisions. How much information to share requires applying judgment on your part. The appropriate amount of information can vary. You need to decide how much and what type of data will help your team vs. what information is unnecessary.

Story: I used to give full debriefs to one of my direct reports. I like having as much information as possible. So, I assumed he would too. I trusted and liked this team member a lot, so I tended to give him even more information than usual. I would tell him company updates, what was happening at our leadership meetings, and the ins and outs of what differing opinions certain people had. One day, he finally interrupted and said, "Emily, I know you're trying to be helpful, but I really would rather just know when a final decision has been made. This other stuff just keeps me up at night." I thought, "Oh! Oh my gosh, I'm sorry! I would never mean to keep you up at night." From then on, I tailored my messaging only to debrief him on critical updates when they were final or very close to being finalized. I only told him what he needed to be aware of.

General Stanley McChrystal has a rule when it comes to sharing information with his troops: "At [the level of a] four-star general [you need to understand] the war is politics. You have people under you to make tactical field maneuvers. At the senior level, if you don't get the politics right, you can't win. [I] Give the people below me enough of the political context, so they understand the environment they're working in. But not too much, so they don't feel too much pressure to be relatively unencumbered."

Does your team know your intent? If you were "killed in action" - perhaps out of the office unexpectedly - what would happen? Do they have enough information to carry out the mission?

Pro Tip: *Do you know your commander's intent? Do you know how you (and your areas of*

> *the business) fit into the overall objective of the company, the board of directors, your constituents? If you don't, go find out.*

Key Takeaways:

- Have bias toward done.
- Protect the asset - and the asset is *you*.
- Be clear on commander's intent.

Key Questions:

- What decision, only you can make, will help the team the most?
- What is the MVP (minimally viable product)?
- What do you have on your calendar this week that protects the asset?

CHAPTER 6

YOUR TEAM

"Never doubt that a small group of thoughtful, committed people can change the world. Indeed. It is the only thing that ever has."

- Margaret Mead

Aptitude and Attitude

There are lots of ways you can measure a team member's performance. Most of what you can look at will fall into two big buckets. One, do they have the hard skills or knowledge to do the job (aptitude)? Examples are GAAP (Generally Applied Accounting Principles) for an accountant or PHP coding proficiency for a developer. Two, is this person a good team member to work with (attitude)? Does this person work collaboratively with team members? Does this person make people's lives easier, not harder?

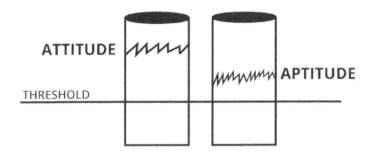

Pay attention to the levels of aptitude and attitude

Ideally, everyone would have a high level of both aptitude and attitude. Most people have one or the other - or more of one than the other. We've probably all come across a person who is very good at his/her job, but is wholly unpleasant to work. When you think of engaging with this person, you cringe and brace yourself. Conversely, there are frequent cases of someone being cheerful and pleasant to be around and tries really, really hard but can't seem to get anything done without a mistake or issue popping up. I've heard this referred to as the "Brilliant Jerk" or "Friendly Incompetent."

A leader should be able to recognize where their team members are on this spectrum.

Top performers have both aptitude and attitude at a high level consistently. If you find someone like this, take note. Make sure you acknowledge and recognize him/her. Look for potential promotion opportunities. Underperformers don't pull their weight in either category - they can't or won't do the job, *and* they have a terrible attitude and can drag the team down. If you notice this happening, then you need to address it. Speak to them, work with them, and give them every opportunity to turn things around. However, if their overall performance doesn't improve, then it's time to transition them out of the organization.

A word of caution, do *not* let someone who has a deficiency in aptitude and attitude stay on your team for too long. In addition to not getting the work done correctly, it sends a horrible signal to the top performers - or even average but dependable performers - about what's allowed. You do not want them thinking, "If they don't see how bad she is, are they paying attention at all?" Or, "If they think that *he's* doing a good job, do they even know what a good job looks like? How are they measuring my performance?"

> **Pro Tip**: *Sometimes, it's tough to tell if someone is not doing something because they can't or because they won't. Here's a blunt but effective way to think about it:*
>
> *Ask yourself, "If their life was on the line, would they be able to perform this task?" If the answer is yes, then they can do it (they know how), but they just choose not to. If the answer is no (they*

> *literally couldn't do it if their life depended on it),*
> *then they don't have the knowledge or capability*
> *to do it. In this case, they may need additional*
> *training. Or if they've had ample training and*
> *just can't get there, their task or role may need to*
> *be passed on to someone else.*

Have a Vision

Good leaders look for the strengths in their team members - both current and *potential* strengths. The best leaders can see the possible but unrealized assets of individuals. It's shocking that many people still see the primary function of a manager or leader as finding mistakes and correcting them. There is a time and place for that, of course. But equally, if not, more importantly, be on the lookout for what they do well. Regularly scan and observe for this. People evolve and grow on their own, and you may miss something if you aren't paying attention - so *actively* be on the lookout.

Very often, a person may not know they are good at something. They may have never thought of themselves in a higher capacity or a higher level. Sometimes, all it takes is for someone else to say it out loud. Something like, "You know you're very good at..." or, "You really shine when you're..." or, "You could run this department one day." Plant a seed and "give them permission" to believe in something about themselves.

It's important not to make false promises. Do not throw something out that people will latch onto and then feel disappointed when it doesn't happen. The threshold for how far to go varies by situation and by person. Do not give compliments just because, only do it if it is real and genuine. If you see something in someone that you believe he/she does not see, then tell this person. Speak life into it. One comment can open new thinking and have a ripple effect that changes someone's life.

> **Quote:** "A good leader is able to paint a picture of a vision for the future and then enlist others to go on the journey with her. A truly conscious leader recognizes that it is not about her, but that the team is looking to her for inspiration and direction."
>
> - Tamra Ryan, CEO

Here is one strategy I like to use with high-potentials. When you're talking to them, casually mention something they do well or that you like, that is *one step ahead of where they are.* Something that is not yet realized, but speak about it as if it has happened or is happening. Expressing this could sound something like, "Yeah, well, I think because you're good at X..." or, "I like when you Y..." or, "When you do Z, that'll put the rest of it in place."

They haven't actually done X, Y, or Z. They are on the cusp of doing it. You saying this aloud may bring it to their awareness in a way they haven't noticed before. Dropping it in the natural flow of conversation like it already *is* - it's already in reality, it's already proven fact - gives them an inherent vote of confidence. They'll step up to meet the expectation.

> **Pro Tip**: *Meet them where they're at. Use this strategy for something one step outside their current capabilities or comfort zone. Don't stretch them too far. Don't take a first-time manager and expect them to perform like a CEO. Flex to wherever they are in their career and development stage.*

A hallmark of a great leader is having a vision for future potential and capabilities and bringing them to life.

Get the Right People in the Right Seats

You may have times when you have *good* people in the organization. They are talented, have the skills the company needs, are a good cultural fit, and work well with everyone. However, they are in the wrong role within the company. They are on the bus but not in the right seat.

Make sure you don't prematurely exit them from the organization *or* keep them too long in a role that they are not suited for. Having this happen can be a loss for the company (they would be more effective in another position) and for the individuals themselves (if they have to wake up and go to a job they don't like every day).

An example of this is a team member who is more suited to back-end, technical work and is in a client-facing, Account Manager type of role. As an Account Manager, communication and project management are vital elements to success. The delivery of the information can be just as important as the actual work done. If a person cannot communicate well over the phone or email, the client experience could be poor.

However, this same person can be an absolute whiz at doing the technical work. Moving this person to an internal, non-client facing role can be a smart move. You can even set up a structure and process to have the technical, subject-matter-expert attend the call and still have an Account Manager run the call and own the overall relationship. It's a win for the client - they always get stellar, top-notch work done as well as a strong point of contact who communicates clearly. It's a win for the individual who is now working in a job he/she is more suited for and enjoys a lot more. Lastly, it's a win for the company, since they have retained top talent.

Don't Assume

Don't assume everyone thinks like you or is motivated by the same things you are. Everyone sees the world through their lens - their background, set of experiences, and biases. There are 7.8 billion people on Earth—all at different points in their lives when they meet you. Expecting everyone to see things the way you do or want what you want is preposterous.

Money is a common motivator. People can be working a job just for the money, which is a perfectly valid reason. Maybe they need money to keep a roof over their head or medicine for a loved one. Perhaps they just like money, and they want more and more of it to buy nice things. Some people might be motivated by the organization's mission and the impact it's having on the world. Others might like their boss or former colleagues, and the chance to work with them again at another organization is what drives them. Sometimes, it's the low-stress factor - maybe they were burning themselves out at their previous job and needed to move to a new role that demanded less of them. Sometimes, a person is of retirement age and has finished their main run and just wants something part-time to keep themselves fresh and on their toes. Sometimes, there's no particular rhyme or reason for someone being in a job other than that they applied for it, got it, and it works just fine for them right now. This list goes on and on, but you get the point. And these are all great and valid reasons for people doing what they do.

The key is knowing what motivates each team member. Trying to figure out what drives people can help you lead and manage them. If you know what they want and can align it to the business's goals, that's the ideal path.

What does this job mean to your team members right now?

Story: *I had someone on my team who was in her early twenties. She dressed casually and was pretty low-key and quiet. She had an entry-level job and worked on a particular project for us and was very good at it. She would dig into large data sets and pick out things that other people didn't see. In my mind, the work was kind of boring and routine. I felt like she was overqualified for it. I assumed she was just too shy to advocate for herself. I saw some untapped potential there and thought, I know I'm going to go to my boss and pitch moving this team member to a new role with higher pay. I was going to surprise the employee with this news. I pictured her face lighting up with gratitude and saying, "Yes, of course. I'd like the new role, and the raise would be awfully nice! Thanks, Emily! You're the best!"*

When I called her to my office and told her, she said, "If you move me, I'll quit." Flabbergasted, I thought, wait, what? After discussing it further, I learned that she had inherited a large sum of money when her parents died unexpectedly. So she didn't care about the money or being promoted. She cared about the specific project. She was interested in the data and liked the work. That's why she applied for the job. Seeing the error of my ways, I reversed the decision to move her and made sure she stayed on that project.

How you figure out each person's motivators will vary. Some people will just tell you without being asked. Some people will tell you, but you'd have to ask first. Others keep their reasons close to their chest. For these people, you will need to be more observant to piece it all together.

Another way to gain insight is to run a personality or behavioral assessment. One of the best I've found is the DISC Assessment. DISC takes a person's observable behaviors and emotions and puts them in a surprisingly - sometimes freakishly - predictable framework. It's in the same family as Myers-Briggs and similar assessments. I like DISC because it is simple, practical and easy to remember. There are only four Styles:

D = Dominance. Tends to be direct, decisive, driven.

I = Influence. Tends to be inspirational, influential, intuitive.

S = Steadiness. Tends to be sincere, steady, sympathetic.

C = Conscientious. Tends to be cautious, concise, correct.

DISC gives you a distinct advantage when interacting and communicating with people. It gives you information about what their strengths are, what they fear, what they want, and how they show up under stress. It teaches you how to communicate with people in the most way effective *for them*.

I usually run a DISC assessment for each of my direct reports, and sometimes their directs too. I'm a DISC practitioner, so I'll run the report and then take them through it. It's incredibly insightful, and people have a lot of fun with it.

If you're interested in having a DISC report run for you or your teams with a debrief session on the specific findings of the report, let me know by contacting me at emily@next-level.coach. See back of the book for how to get a free report.

If you'd like to learn more about the DISC methodology and don't want to read a textbook or stuffy definition, read *Taking Flight*. It is a fun and easy read (can finish it in a weekend). It explains the four DISC Styles through a story about four birds solving a problem in their forest. The four bird types are an Eagle, Parrot, Dove, and Owl, which correspond with the four DISC Styles.

What to Do With Complainers

It's *easy* to complain. It's the path of least resistance. It's the easy way out.

If someone on your team is complaining *more than helping find solutions*, then they don't belong on your team. Period. Another way to think of it is if their overall contribution to the group is a *net negative*, and they are hurting you more than helping you, then it's time for them to move on.

> **Pro Tip**: *There is a time and place for venting. It's natural, and everyone needs to do it from time to time. Part of your job as a leader is to create that space for your team members when appropriate. Just make sure this is the exception, not the rule.*

Key Takeaways:

- Two big buckets of performance evaluation are aptitude and attitude.
- Have a vision for what could be but not yet is.
- Don't assume people's motivators - ask or find out.

Key Questions:

- Which team members are making a net positive contribution? Which are making a net negative contribution?
- Where is the untapped potential on your team and how can you help them realize it?
- What motivates and drives your team members to do what they do?

CHAPTER 7

COMMUNICATION

"The art of communication is the language of leadership."

- James Humes

Verbal Processors vs. Internal Thinkers

Just like motivators, people process information differently as well. Some people think by talking out loud to others, and others think in their head. Neither one is good or bad or better than the other; they are just different. However, not picking up on which one you are and which one the person you're working with is, can cause communication wires to get crossed.

Internal thinkers may mull a decision or a topic over this way and then that way in their head. They'll think through all the pros and cons, the trade-offs, all the options and any other considerations they can think of. They will *then* talk to other people and get different opinions and perspectives.

Verbal processors think by talking out loud to people or themselves. Hearing the words out loud helps them think through a decision or topic. They will bounce ideas off another person right away. Their train of thought might seem random and be full of non-sequiturs. After speaking with people, they might talk to a different group or think about it themselves. Or they might just make the decision right there and then because they've done their thinking.

If you're a verbal processor, make sure your out-loud thinking isn't taken as gospel. One of my previous bosses was a verbal processor and also had a very authoritative-sounding voice. To make it clear when he wanted to just soundboard ideas, he would say, "This isn't a directive, I'm just thinking out loud here," so no one would leave the meeting and go *do* something.

If you're an internal thinker, make sure your team knows that your silence isn't because you weren't listening or don't care or are afraid to answer. Let them know where you're at, "Great discussion, some good information here from all sides. I'm going to think this through and get back to you." If appropriate, talk through some of your initial thoughts about *how* you're going to be thinking about the issue or idea. After the subsequent rounds of thinking, it's helpful to explain how you reached the final decision. You're not justifying your decision - but the gap between when someone last heard from you when you were just starting to think about something and the final decision might seem wide. It may be helpful to explain to them the reasoning behind how you got there.

Story: *There was a brainstorming meeting with a dozen people. The person leading the meeting and the majority of participants were verbal processors. This made for a very lively and engaged discussion during the session. One person sat quietly throughout the conference, only saying a few things here and there. The leader noticed this and was a little concerned the person wasn't understanding or was intimidated to speak. The leader made sure to give the person opportunities to speak. The person only gave short answers. The meeting ended. The next day, the person who had been quiet during the meeting came to the leader and told the leader about an idea. It blew all the other ideas out of water. The leader got so excited and then said, "Why didn't you say bring this idea up in the meeting yesterday?" The person said, "I didn't have it yet. I had to think about it."*

Subtle Nuance vs. a 2x4

How people *receive* information is another key part of communication to pay attention to. Don't assume everyone receives information the way you do. I almost always pick up on the nuances of people's communication – the content, what they're saying, what they're not saying, their word choice intonation of their voice, their body language. Naturally, this was my default way of giving feedback to people when I first became a manager. Sometimes, it would work beautifully. I was able to convey what needed to be done differently without rattling a person. Other times, it seemed not to register at all.

On the flip side, if you have a loud, boisterous, and direct personality or voice, you may need to dial it down when giving feedback to specific team members. What seems like a perfectly reasonable conversation to you, might feel like someone screaming at them through a megaphone. You might inadvertently send them into a tailspin. A misplaced and misdelivered offhand comment of yours could have them ruminating over it for hours or days. Soften or lighten your message and delivery when needed for the most effective results.

Story: One of the best coaches I've had was an instructor at the coaching organization I received my training. I remember her explaining this concept in terms of coaching style for various clients. She recounted how she had to learn to change her delivery when *working with some clients. Her default communication style is straightforward. Laughing, she said, "I'm from New York, born and raised, and I have a big loud family. So if you didn't speak up or get to the point, no one would hear you. I'm actually known as the quiet one in my family." This coach said she never knew she was too loud or direct until she met people from different parts of the country and world. But over her long and successful coaching career, she has picked up on the fact she needed to flex to a softer communication style for specific clients.*

Pro Tip: To see a fantastic and hilarious example of giving feedback in a different way than you're used to, watch the movie A League of Their Own. Tom Hanks plays Jimmy Dugan, the coach of a women's baseball team during World War II.

He has two scenes where he lets a player know she missed the "cut off man" - when throwing the ball from far away in the outfield to home plate, you want to throw it to a teammate in the middle, so the ball relays faster.

In the first scene, he delivers feedback to the player in the same way he does in a men's game. He shouts and screams at the player and she starts sobbing. This elicits the famous line, "Are you crying? Are you crying? There's no crying.

> There's no crying in baseball!" He then gets into a scuffle with the umpire for making his player cry, and gets kicked out of the game.
>
> In the second scene, later in the movie, the same player misses the cutoff man again, and he has to give her that same feedback. But he doesn't want to make her cry or get kicked out of the game, so he has to change up the way he conveys the information. With an enormous amount of effort, he forces a smile and in a light tone, he sputters out the words while visibly shaking, "Say, Evelyn. You, you ...you're still missing the cut off man...Now, now...that is something...I'd like you to work on before next season." It's one of the funniest scenes in the movie.

And vs. But, Why vs. How

Switching out one little word can have a significant impact on the message you're conveying. Changing a word can, of course, change the entire meaning of a statement. "I will not share your data" vs. "I will share your data." There also can be more nuanced differences having to do with connotation or perception of what you're saying - how a statement "lands" with the listener.

Two common swaps are useful especially when providing feedback.

The first swap is "and" and "but." Many people will give feedback by laying out a list of positive things and then say "but" and deliver negative feedback. Doing so can cancel out or negate everything you said before "but" with many listeners. If you simply replace the "but" with an "and," it can change the dynamic of your sentence.

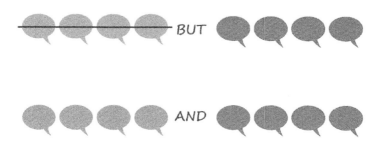

Using the word "but" can sound like everything said previously is negated. Use the word "and" instead when appropriate.

Pro Tip: You can also just end a sentence and start a new one with no transition. Doing this can feel a bit awkward at first. People tend to speak with lots of filler and transition words. With a little awareness and practice, it can be a handy tool.

The second swap is "what" instead of "why." Using the word "why" can make someone feel like they are being attacked and taps into their emotional side. If someone is feeling defensive, it's tough to have a productive conversation. In comparison, using a "what" question can feel less personal. It's more logical - it's talking about an action or behavior, not about them as a person. It tends to be received more rationally and calmly - this clear-headedness is more conducive to a meaningful conversation.

Ask vs. Tell

Using a question instead of demand can make all the difference in getting what you want. Most people don't like being told what to do, especially when they have no choice or feel like it's an ultimatum.

There are times as a leader when you have to tell someone to do something. However, a useful trick is making the statement a question. Now, both you and the other person may know very well that the answer is going to be yes. But it can land a whole hell of a lot better. Think about being on the receiving end of:

"Do this…" vs. "Would you be able to…"

"Give me …" vs. "Any way you can…"

If you can get the thing you want accomplished with less drama, push back, or resentment, go that route.

Using a question vs. a statement is particularly useful when a "mistake" or "error" has occurred.

When you first hear of an "emergency" or a considerable problem someone caused, don't assume you have all the facts. You usually don't. *Ask* the question.

Ask yourself - "What is the best way I can verify this information?"

Ask others - "I hear X, Y, Z, do you have any information on this from your end? What are your thoughts on what happened?"

If you confirm an error has occurred, turn blame into a request with a question.

- "There must have been a really good reason for this decision. Can you walk me through your criteria and thought process?"
- "I've just learned about a recent decision. I'm always interested in hearing how people are going about this. What were the criteria and factors that lead up to the decision?"
- "I noticed the monthly reports didn't go out to our customers. Those usually go out every month on the 3rd. It's part of our service deliverable. Can you run me through your approach on the monthly reports?"

Remember, we've all slipped up. When you've made a mistake, what is the last thing you'd want to hear from someone? I told you so. Most people - and especially top performers - are usually beating themselves up already. Some of them self-flagellate pretty hard, and piling more on will do zero good.

Instead, the two main things you want to get are: (1) what happened to cause the problem so you can prevent it from happening again, and (2) come to a mutual agreement on the next steps going forward.

Pro Tip: *Honestly, ask the question and be open to any answer. Don't already have your next statement locked and loaded no matter what they say. Set the stage for an honest, inviting, and productive conversation. Do not make anyone feel like they've been sent to the principal's office.*

Key Takeaways:

- Pay attention to how you are delivering information (it can be as important or more important than the content of what you're saying).
- Take time to understand how you and your team prefer to communicate.
- Ask questions to seek out or confirm data when appropriate (vs. making statements or demands).

Key Questions:

- How do you and your team process information best?
- What part of your communication style can you switch up to get better results?
- What is a statement that could be turned into a question?

CHAPTER 8

PRACTICAL AND TACTICAL

"It's the little details that are vital. Little things make big things happen."

- John Wooden

Recruiting and hiring

There are hundreds of books on the recruiting and hiring process. I won't cover the usual topics here even though this is one of my favorite things to do. And if you need help with recruiting and hiring, please contact me (emily@nextlevel.coach); I'd be more than happy to help. Seriously, I love this stuff.

I will give you some quick high-level items to keep in mind. Then, I'll give you numerous "little" things that most people miss and don't get covered. These will give you an advantage and a higher probability of making good hiring decisions.

Three key, high-level items:

Firstly, who you bring onto your team is one of the most important decisions you'll make as a leader. It's also one of the most difficult. There are so many variables and unknowns when you make a hire. If half the people you hire turn out to be good hires, you're doing well. Yes, that's right, 50%. Hiring is challenging. Don't beat yourself up too badly if you hire someone who doesn't work out. But do all you can upfront to put the odds in your favor, especially with senior roles. The more senior the position in the organization, the more in-depth the vetting process should be.

Secondly, use the aptitude and attitude buckets mentioned in previous chapters as a framework for evaluating candidates. As you collect information during the interview process, what level of aptitude and attitude are you seeing? The candidate should have the hard skill-set to do the job and fit in well with the team and company culture. Both of these are equally important. Someone could have the necessary skills and just not be the right fit for the team or company. They would be unsuccessful in the role. Nothing wrong with the candidate, nothing wrong with the team or company. Just not a good fit.

Thirdly, if a candidate looks "good on paper" and by every outward measure he/she did well in the interviews, but something just doesn't feel quite right, pay attention to that! You may be working with this person day-in and day-out for a very long time. Either get the information you need to quell the uneasy feeling - from your interview notes, conversations with colleagues, references, or a follow-up call with the candidate. If it still doesn't pass your gut check, don't make an offer. *Pay attention to your spidey-sense.*

The "little" things:

From the moment a candidate engages with your company, everything he/she does is fair game for scrutiny. This also goes in the reverse direction as well. From the moment you contact the candidate, he/she will - or should - pay attention to how you interact with him/her.

I vet for the big things like experience, background, desired compensation, location, etc., of course. But I also set up the process to collect as many data points on "little things" as I can. This is where you can get a real sense of how a person operates and what it would be like to work with this person.

Resume

Content, and formatting. Spelling and presentation matters. The threshold for what "good" is will depend on the role - an accountant and marketing manager may have very different looking resumes. But the basics need to be covered. I once had a candidate who listed his "pubic speaking" as a top skill and then mentioned his keen attention to detail. I passed on his resume. I wish him all the best with his public speaking engagements.

Job board questions

If you have the opportunity to add questions into a job recruiting tool or platform (like ZipRecruiter or Indeed), take it. You can select the typical questions like: "Are you willing to undergo a background check, in accordance with local law and regulations?" or "Do you have the following license or certification?" etc. But I also like to add a custom question. I use the free-text box format for the answer. This one should be an "easy" or straight-forward question that they don't have to think about too hard. Don't make the candidate write a novel back to you at this stage. I also make it optional.

Here, you can even have a question with a one-character reply. For example, "On a scale of 1-10, how would you rate your knowledge on…"

This simple question can garner many different types of responses—each giving a little insight into the candidate.

- Most people just enter a number. Which is great, step one accomplished - they read, understood, and answered the question.

- Some people enter a range, also sufficient if the range is close together (i.e., "7-8"). It gets a little weird when they enter a broad range (i.e., "6-10") - there's a pretty big difference there, which is it?

- I look at the actual answer, of course. I had someone write, "If 1 is the worst, I'd give myself a 1." Another time, I had someone list "19." I did not move forward with either candidate.

- Sometimes you'll get an oddball answer like a fraction 8.77777. Which may or may not be fine depending on how quirky someone in the role can be.

- Some people will write a short explanation as to why they gave themself the score they did, "I'll say a 9 because there is always more to learn." This gives you a little insight into their thinking.

- A few folks will write paragraphs back to you - remember I intentionally keep the answer format long-form text so they can do this. I usually pass on people who write me the sequel to *War and Peace* in their job board questionnaire answer. I asked for a one number rating, are you able to do this? Can you answer concisely and to the point?

- Some people will use this answer box to explain something about their application information. For example, if the job listing is in Seattle, Washington, and they live somewhere else, they might let me know they are relocating to Seattle next month. Information like this is useful to have and shows they are thinking through their information from the hiring manager's perspective.

Another type of question to ask is an opinion question. These are still relatively easy and straight-forward as there is no right or wrong answer - it's *their* opinion.

For example, "What is the difference between an average salesperson and a great one?"

- Here, I look at spelling and grammar, especially if they're in a client-facing role. You would be *amazed* at how many people can't put a coherent sentence together (reminder: this requires both a noun and a verb). Many people do not capitalize the first word in a sentence or misspell words. I discard all of these answers.
- I look at the content of their answers. Here, I'm very flexible. As long as they don't say something completely asinine or extreme, I move them

through. My net is still cast pretty wide at this stage. I don't have to agree 100% with their answer. I asked for their opinion, and they gave it to me.

- I look at how much they wrote. Most people will write 2-3 sentences; that's all I'm looking for. If they write a little more with an opinion question, that's great. If it's a great wall of text that I have to scroll down, then it is probably a little much.

- I also pick out if their answer is about the mental side of things or the tactical side. For example, do they mention something like perseverance or how they organize their activity tracking spreadsheet? Both entirely satisfactory answers; it just adds a data point.

- I look for if they give a cliched answer or an original one. Both are fine at this stage, but I prefer an original one. It shows the person either took time to think about the question or they actually have this knowledge from their experience.

- Many people will not answer the optional question at all. I pass on these. If you don't take 30 seconds to fill out an answer, you don't want this job badly enough.

Preliminary questions

This step is one of the most useful I've come across for evaluating candidates. A colleague told me about this when I was hiring to fill numerous roles across the company, and my calendar was out of control. Using preliminary questions is a huge time saver. It's also another excellent way to collect valuable data points. I typically use these types of questions after the resume and job board answer review and before the initial phone interview.

Another quick note, initially, I thought a low percentage of candidates would answer these questions, and I'd lose too many candidates at this step. I was wrong. Almost everyone replied.

Pick 3-5 questions and number them in the body of the email after your greeting and opening sentences. The questions can change depending on the role. I'd suggest still keeping some of these relatively "easy." Be respectful of the candidates' time. Here are some examples: "Are you able to work core business hours in your time zone?", "Can you confirm you reviewed the salary range posted for this position?" or, "Are you able to reliably commute to the office location?" Then, for some roles, I might add something like, "What is your leadership style? I know this is a broad question, one or two sentences is fine." Something like this will work as well: "What strategies or tools do you use to stay organized?" or "What is one way to organize an inbox?"

I read the content of the answers, of course. But you also get a slew of little data points coming in. Some will reply within an hour; some will take weeks. Some will have a greeting at the beginning of the email; some will simply answer the questions. Some will number their answers back; some will just write paragraphs. Some will convey warmth and excitement in their email; some will be more aloof and distant.

Initial phone call

- First, I listen to how they answer the telephone. I cannot tell you how many people pick up and respond with "Hello" with either a surprised or rude tone. If you know an interview call is coming in at a specific date and time, how you don't answer the phone with proper etiquette is beyond me. The group of candidates that nails this greeting most often are salespeople. "Good afternoon, this is Jack," "Hello, this is so and so is that Emily?", "Hi, Emily!" These are all great ways to pick up and answer the phone for an interview.

- If I am interviewing a candidate for a client-facing role, I'll usually throw in some questions they probably won't be able to answer. They will inevitably run into these scenarios with customers, and I want to see how well they say, "I don't know."

- Listen for their ability to listen. I always listen to how well the candidate is listening to me. I'll give whomever I'm speaking with information about the company and what I'm looking for with the role throughout the conversation. A strong candidate will pick up on those and weave those back into the conversation. Either using my word or phrasing or just indicating by what they are saying that they heard and understood something that was said previously. I love these candidates. The opposite is a red flag - if they ask a question that I've already answered or don't listen to any of my questions and seem to be answering pre-canned answers - this is something I note.

- I'll also drop pieces of information about myself that they can build rapport around - where I grew up, went to school, what I watch on TV, hobbies, etc. Good client-facing folks, and especially salespeople, will pick up on those and comment on them to build rapport.

- At the end of the phone interview, I'll ask "What questions do you have for me?" If there are *none*, that's a red flag. If they are all about the salary and PTO that might be a yellow flag. If there is a mix of what the company culture is, what success in the role looks like, what challenges the company may face in the next year or two, the benefits package then that's usually a good sign.

Thank you notes

- Writing a thank-you note or email takes under a minute. It literally can be 2-3 sentences. I probably get less than 5% of candidates who write me any thank-you note after an interview. These stand out.

Skills tests

- If there's any sort of skills test you can give, I'd highly recommend it. This is in case people can "talk the talk" really well but can't do the technical work you need them to do.

Fit interviews

- I'd strongly recommend "fit" interviews with other team members. These can be colleagues from another department who the candidate will work with or just someone in the organization you trust and respect their opinion. They will give you useful insights into aspects of the candidate that you might not have seen during your interactions. It also allows the candidate to meet other people in the company and get a sense of the culture. They must have enough information to make an informed decision too.

- When selecting which team members will be in the fit interview loop, I try to represent either people the candidate is going to work with or someone opposite in personality or temperament from the candidate. Can they "flex" and work with different kinds of people? Sometimes you'll have fit interviews scheduled with one team member at a time. Alternatively, you can set up a panel interview - so a candidate is speaking with multiple team members at once.

Story: *I was part of a panel fit interview for a sales leader role, and our CEO had put three people on the panel with a wide variety of personality types. On one side of the spectrum was an outgoing, talkative, stylish Vice President, and on the other side was a very quiet, very methodical Director of IT who had three go-to outfits that involved rotating T-shirts. I was in the middle - figuratively and literally. Our CEO did this because he noticed that this salesperson used the "mirroring" technique - where you pick up on the temperament, personality, and pace of the person you're speaking with and try to match it. People tend to like people who are like them, and this can work quite well. Our boss wanted to see what the salesperson would do if he had three very different types of people in front of him and if he could "flex" to each.*

How do they treat the receptionist?

- In one of my previous jobs, we had one entry door to the lobby, and everyone that came in spoke with the receptionist sitting at the front desk. I'd always ask her how the candidates were when they first came in. If she said they were rude to her, it was a data point. For example, after one person signed in, she said he tossed the pen back at her instead of handing it to her or setting in on the counter. Another person hit on her. These were no hires.

What time do they arrive?

- To me, you should walk through the door ten minutes early. You *definitely* should not be late. Showing you have your stuff together enough to arrive on time is important. But I've had candidates show up an *hour* early. To me, this also shows a lack of awareness. I make them wait until our scheduled time.

Remember interviews can make people nervous - really nervous

- This may seem like an obvious point, but when you've interviewed lots of people, it's a good reminder. People show nervousness in different ways. I remember one candidate I interviewed was so nervous his voice cracked a couple of times, and his hands visibly shook. When he handed me a copy of his resume (kudos to him for bringing an extra copy), the paper waved all around. He ended up being one of our top data analysts. I've had others laugh uncontrollably. Others will sweat - I take affinity with these people because I do this as well when nervous. Putting them at ease is an art. I usually talk for a little bit just to get them used to being in the interview, and then I'll ask some super softball questions - "Did you find the office ok?" or, "What did you do this weekend?" Even something like, "I'm still getting over the (enter a recent news story here)."

> **Pro Tip:** *On rare occasions, if someone is extremely nervous and I can't shake them out of it, I'll do something self-deprecating like "accidentally" knocking over my coffee cup or water bottle. This breaks the ice and the "we're in an interview setting" mentality - I get up and get some paper towels and clean it up and apologize to them. It reminds them they're just talking to a person who can be clumsy and knock things over.*

How do they handle a reschedule?

- Sometimes I will have to reschedule an interview, or they will ask for a reschedule. How they handle or communicate this is a great data point.

Follow-up

- If we agreed on a follow-up item, how quickly do they follow-up? For example, if they say they're going to send me the link to their portfolio to see some samples of their work tomorrow, do they do it?

Unplanned call

- For a director role or above, I'll call the candidate when we do not have a planned call. I make this call sometime later in the interview process. I do this after the skills test, my interview, and fit interviews, when we've established some sort of rapport. I listen for how well they handle the call - do they sound or act the same as in the interview. Even if they can't talk right then, how do they tell me? If it goes to voicemail, what does the voicemail prompt sound like and when do they respond to my call?

References

- Of course, references are going to give the candidate glowing reviews. They've been handpicked by the candidate. But I try to build enough rapport with them at the beginning of the call to be able to ask some meaningful questions towards the end. I like, "If Sara got the role, what advice would you give me to make sure I set her up for success?" With a question like that, they can throw in things that might be weaknesses but put in this light, are helpful suggestions to make their candidate successful.

Remember interviewing is a two-way street

- Candidates are evaluating you and the company as well.
- Represent yourself and the company well from the beginning all the way to end when you decline a candidate.
    - Send a carefully worded email letting them know they did not get the position.
    - I've written emails to candidates who didn't get the role but were very good. I told them what they did well and what they could do better during the interview process. You'd be amazed at how much these are appreciated even though they didn't get the job.
    - If a candidate was a finalist for a position, I would offer him/her a call if he/she wanted to get some feedback on why we went another direction.

Vet harder when under pressure

I've made some of the worst hires when I'm under pressure to get someone in quickly. In these situations, you need to slow down and make sure you go through all the steps in your process without cutting corners.

Do not, I repeat, do not lower your standards. Don't discard data that's staring you in the face or make excuses for any data points you wouldn't otherwise overlook - avoid saying, "Oh yeah, that's not really that big a deal. I think it will be ok," or, "Hey, I need a warm body, and she's got a pulse; get her in here." Lowering your standards will come back to bite you. Don't do it.

Asking the right questions:

> **Quote**: *"My mother made me a scientist without ever intending to.*
>
> *Every other Jewish mother in Brooklyn would ask her child after school: 'So? Did you learn anything today?'*
>
> *But not my mother.*
>
> *'Izzy,' she would say, 'did you ask a good question today?'*
>
> *That difference — asking good questions — made me become a scientist."*
>
> *- Isidor ("Izzy") Rabi*

It's more important to ask the right question than have the right answer.

Are you asking the right questions?

Leaders are often looked to and thought of for having "the right answer," "all the answers," or "the final answer."

In asking the most relevant question, you get the most suitable answer. The premise of a question can cause you (or the person you're asking) to think about a problem in a new way. How you frame up a situation can lead to new or better solutions and ideas.

Don't spend hours or days solving the wrong problem - or answering the wrong question.

Questions are so important, that is why I've included key questions at the end of each chapter. I've listed them together in the Key Questions section in the back of the book. There are some other sample questions for common scenarios leaders may face as well. Having some of these at the top of mind and ready to deploy will make you more effective.

I suggest that you get a notebook and write down three questions at the top of separate pages. Pick the three most relevant to you right now. Then, write out your answers, thoughts, or whatever comes up for you on each page. You can come back and reference this chapter and the list of questions as many times as you need in the future.

Key Takeaways:

- Recruiting and hiring is one of the most important jobs of a leader. Make sure you have a strong vetting process and pay attention to the "little" things that give you key insights.

- Having the right question is more important than having the right answer. Pay attention to the kinds of questions you're asking (to yourself and others).

- Write down or think through some questions you want to be asking this next week.

Key Questions:

- What are some ways you can gain more information and insight about candidates in the recruiting and hiring process?

- What are some ways you can remember to ask a question instead of making a statement when appropriate?

- What is the most *relevant* question (in this scenario)?

CONCLUSION

"I want to be a better leader."

"If I just had more confidence...".

"I need to manage my time better."

These are common refrains I hear from so many people. I've said them myself many times too.

All of these require work and the willingness to invest in the process, the progress towards the goal, and in yourself. *You have done that.* Know that you have done that and by reading this book. You have proven you're the type of person who is constantly reaching to grow and improve. Well done!

Remember, craft your framework, turn failure into progress, and optimize all your experiences into learning and insight.

This knowledge and knowing you're able to draw on multiple resources will make you a more confident decision-maker. Replace worry with wisdom. Remember to be on the lookout for these opportunities.

You are now equipped to review your belief set and know how much it impacts your actions and choices. If you do the work to find out which contact lenses you currently have on, you can ask yourself, "Better 1 or better 2?" and flip lenses at will.

Put together your own personal playbook and run a routine of excellence every day. Allow this to evolve with you over time.

Use the business lessons, practical and tactical strategies, and tools to help your team and organization run more effectively and efficiently.

There is a lot of information in this book. I'd suggest, working on one or two things at a time. Take a few minutes to write out some notes, such as your thinking around a topic now or the action steps you're going to take. Focus on them for a few weeks or months. Re-read the chapter or section about the topic. Then, add any quick notes and insights from your experience.

I've worked on all of the things discussed in this book myself. I continue to work on them every day. I've been through the ups and downs of business, management, team dynamics, etc. As I have taken on new roles throughout the years I have built up my leadership style – and continue to refine it.

Here is my encouragement to you: *You can do this.*

You *can* become the leader you want to be. You can step up and rise to the occasion. Do the work. It might not happen overnight, but small wins will add up faster than you think. Time will pass anyway. Who do you want to be in a week, in a month, in a year? Start today. It will be worth it.

> **Quote**: *"I didn't say it would be easy. I said it would be the truth."*
>
> *- Morpheus*

> **Quote**: *"I didn't say it would be easy, I said it would be worth it."*
>
> *- Emily Sander*

Key Questions

Below is a handy collection of key questions from the previous chapters:

Chapter 1 - "FAILURE"

- What would you do today if you knew you couldn't fail?
- What will let you know you're at the bottom of the loop?
- What go-to strategies or tools will you use to loop up?

Chapter 2 - SWIZZLE

- What areas can you leverage for swizzling?
- What will you do to apply them in your own way?
- Are there any themes or patterns you see come up across different areas?

Chapter 3 – CONTACT LENS

- What lenses are you looking through now?
- Are they serving you well (or causing more harm than good)?
- What do you want your lenses and belief set to be going forward?

Chapter 4 - PLAYBOOK

- What playbook or system is best suited to your strengths and style?
- Which play calls would you benefit the most from adding to your playbook?
- Which play calls would you like to stop running?

Chapter 5 - YOU AS A LEADER

- What decision, only you can make, will help the team the most?
- What is the MVP (minimally viable product)?
- What do you have on your calendar this week that protects the asset?

Chapter 6 - YOUR TEAM

- Which team members are making a net positive contribution? Which are making a net negative contribution?
- Where is the untapped potential on your team and how can you help them realize it?
- What motivates and drives your team members to do what they do?

Chapter 7 - COMMUNICATION

- How do you and your team process information best?

- What part of your communication style can you switch up to get better results?
- What is a statement that could be turned into a question?

Chapter 8 - PRACTICAL AND TACTICAL

- What are some ways you can gain more information and insight about candidates in the recruiting and hiring process?
- What are some ways you can remember to ask a question instead of making a statement when appropriate?
- What is the most *relevant* question (in this scenario)?

Sample questions

Questions to ask when making decisions or weighing options:

1. What is Option A? What is Option B?
2. What door does this open? What does this make possible?
3. What door does this close? What does this make impossible?
4. What is the opportunity cost? What am I giving up by doing this (time, money, energy, sanity, etc)?
5. How much am I assuming or guessing (surrounding this decision)? Is it worth checking?

6. What would some alternatives look like?
7. Do I need to make this decision *now*?
8. If I had to make this decision this second, what is my gut saying to do?
9. Is this decision irreversible, or can it be easily adjusted later?
10. What would be a bias towards action?

Questions to ask when prioritizing and managing your time:

1. Am I being productive or just being busy?
2. Do I know my top 1-3 priorities right now? Can I say them out loud to myself (or other people)?
3. Are my activities/actions aligned with these 1-3 goals?
4. If I looked at my calendar for the past week or month, would it reflect my top priorities? What if I looked ahead to the next week or month?
5. Am I spending time where I'm at my highest contribution?
6. What do I need to let go of?
7. Does this require more *thinking* or more *doing*?
8. Is my scope for this too broad?
9. What is one thing I can remove to improve my life, prioritization, and production?
10. If I had half the time I have now (fewer days in the week, fewer hours in the day), what would still bubble

to the top of the priority list and what would fall away?

Questions to ask yourself:

1. What is my definition of success?
2. *How will I know* I'm successful?
3. How do I measure success?
4. Is this the best way to measure it? Is it still the most appropriate way to look at it?
5. What do I need more of, what do I need less of?
6. What do I need to give myself a break on/more slack on?
7. What is my vision of myself as a leader? As a…?
8. What am I learning? What am I learning about myself?
9. What is in my control? What action can I take right now?
10. Who am I in my own story right now?

Questions to empower others:

1. What do you think?
2. Can you tell me more about…?
3. What about…is important to you?
4. What does…mean to you?
5. How can I help support your success?

Request

Can you help? If you liked this book and found it helpful, could you please take a brief moment to review it on Amazon?

Reviews are extremely important to the success of a book! So if you've liked what you've read, please take two minutes to help me out with a review. THANK YOU!

I'd appreciate any feedback. As a big thank you for your review, email emily@nextlevel.coach with a link to your verified review and receive a free 60-minute coaching session.

ABOUT AUTHOR

Emily Sander has spent more than fifteen years in the business world. She's built global teams from the ground up, accelerated growth at establish businesses, and been hired to "smoke jump into dumpster fires" and turn around dysfunctional teams.

When she realized that her favorite role was mentoring leaders, she decided to pursue coaching. As a C-Suite executive and an ICF-Certified coach, she combines her experience and proven insights with a keen ability to understand each client's unique personality and situation.

HIGHLIGHTS

SIGN UP FOR A COACHING SESSION

INTERESTED IN COACHING?

Email me at **emily@nextlevel.coach**, reference book code NEXTLEVELBOOK.

Receive a **60% discount** off any coaching package.

ORDER A DISC REPORT

Email me at emily@nextlevel.coach, reference book code NEXTLEVELDISC. Receive a **free** DISC report.

For my recommended reading list for leaders
visit my site for descriptions and links:
https://nextlevel.coach/resources

Made in the USA
Coppell, TX
24 April 2021

54446036R00115